A Competency Based Approach
to Training and Development

Financial Times Management Briefings are happy to receive proposals from individuals who have expertise in the field of management education.

If you would like to discuss your ideas further, please contact Andrew Mould, Commissioning Editor.

Tel: 0171 447 2210
Fax: 0171 240 5771
e-mail: andrew.mould@pitmanpub.co.uk

FINANCIAL TIMES
Management Briefings

Human Resources

A Competency Based Approach to Training and Development

BERNARD WYNNE

DAVID STRINGER

London • Hong Kong • Johannesburg • Melbourne • Singapore • Washington DC

PITMAN PUBLISHING
128 Long Acre, London WC2E 9AN
Tel: +44 (0)171 447 2000
Fax: +44 (0)171 240 5771

A Division of Pearson Professional Limited

First published in Great Britain 1997

© Pearson Professional Limited 1997

The right of B. Wynne and D. Stringer to be identified as
authors of this work has been asserted by them in accordance
with the Copyright, Designs, and Patents Act 1988.

ISBN 0 273 63173 X

British Library Cataloguing in Publication Data
A CIP catalogue record for this book can be obtained from the British Library.

10 9 8 7 6 5 4 3 2 1

Printed and bound in Great Britain

The Publishers' policy is to use paper manufactured from sustainable forests.

CONTENTS

About the authors

Bernard Wynne is Principal of Bernard Wynne Associates and Director of the European Mentoring Centre.

Following a background in human resource management and development in financial services, Bernard moved into consultancy in 1988. He was a Director of the ITEM Group plc before establishing Bernard Wynne Associates in 1994.

He consults widely in the areas of HR, communications, management development, performance management and performance improvement through quality and customer service in the public and private sector. He has considerable experience of working with managers in skill development in Europe, Asia and North America.

He writes extensively on HR and management development topics and is the Author of a previous guide in the Technical Communications series – *Performance Appraisal: a practical guide to appraising the performance of employees*.

He has contributed chapters to:
The Handbook of Training and Development, on Evaluation of Training and
The Handbook of Management Development, on Coaching and Mentoring.

Bernard Wynne Associates: 180 Blackfen Road, Sidcup, Kent DA15 8PT
Tel: 0181 850 6458   Fax: 0181 850 8974

David Stringer founded Momentum business and training partnership in 1992.

Following a successful career in sales and management of financial services, he became Group Sales Training Manager for one of the UK's major financial institutions. Promotion to Assistant Training Manager, then specific responsibility for people and performance improvement across 12 diverse subsidiaries, coupled with experience of working with one of the world's leading business consultancies, provided the background for forming Momentum, which delivers consultancy and training services to clients in the public and private sectors in Europe and Asia.

He consults widely in the areas of sales and sales management competencies, the management of careers and a wide range of management skills. He was the architect of a multi-media package 'Coaching to Improve Performance', a core element of a programme which won a UK National Training Award in 1993.

An accomplished presenter, David has spoken at events throughout Britain and Asia, ranging from small workshops to major conferences. He has a wide involvement in media relations, including a number of published articles and broadcasts.

Momentum business & training partnership: PO Box 433, Orpington, Kent BR6 9WJ
Tel: 01689 898582   Fax: 01689 898085

1   Finding your way around the competency maze – an introduction

What are Competencies?

A whole industry has grown out of the quest to define competencies and their use in organisations. For over a decade, the glossary has been growing and the jargon becoming ever more mystifying.

Many operational managers have been put off by the proliferation of jargon, in just the same way that a generation before them were deterred by the new language of Information Technology. This perception is particularly regrettable, because competencies link the person to the job in a more robust way than ever before.

Put simply, competencies are:

> **The things people have to be, know and do,**
> **to achieve the outputs required in their job.**

In our research, one respondent expressed the issue for him, at an individual level, as a particularly poignant question:

> **"What do I need to be good at, to be good at my job?"**

There are almost as many definitions of competencies as there are researchers and practitioners. In the UK, the tendency is to relate to job outputs, whereas in the USA most refer to job inputs. That is:

- Outputs-related: measuring competencies in relation to whether an employee meets or exceeds work standards and expectations.

- Inputs-related: reflecting the knowledge, skills and attitudes that affect the employee's ability to perform.

Both approaches have merit, but we have found it easier to define and measure outputs-related competencies. Most employees are measured and rewarded (or should be) in respect of their actual value to the organisation, not their intrinsic value.

We have provided our own definition below, which will underpin the remainder of this report.

A Definition of Competencies

We believe that organisations need to agree for themselves what they mean by competencies so that the application can be designed to be understandable and usable by all. Therefore as a working definition we propose:

'Competencies represent the accumulated skills, knowledge, behaviour and attitude which individuals apply in achieving the outputs required in their job.'

This means that competencies need to cover the skills, attitudes and behaviours which apply to all jobs in an organisation, and also the professional and technical skills and knowledge which apply within specific jobs and professions within organisations.

In preparing this report we have restricted ourselves mainly to considering those competencies of a generic nature which we believe could apply to all jobs. The application of a competency approach to the professional and technical elements of work are organisation specific and therefore need to be considered and developed by organisations for themselves.

The practical examples used throughout the text are examples of competencies which can most effectively be applied to management, supervisory and administrative jobs. The process we describe can, of course, be adapted for use in defining and applying competencies across a range of jobs in any organisation.

Why Should I be Interested in Competencies?

As a Business Manager:

A competency-based approach to your people has many advantages, from recruitment, through development, to promotion, succession and career management, encompassing all areas of performance management. Being outputs and results oriented, attention remains focused on your primary business needs, throughout. You should be able to recruit, measure and manage your people more objectively and effectively, and be more sure that you will be able to place the right person in the right place, at the right time.

As an Individual Manager or Employee:

You may be reasonably sure that, sooner or later, judgements will be made about you, based on your competencies. Job mobility, within or outside your organisation, is likely to become the norm. It will become increasingly important for you to:

- understand the background and application of competencies

- be able accurately to define your own competencies in your current job

- establish what competencies are required in the next job/s you may be seeking

- then plan to develop your competencies in line with your aspirations.

As an HR/HRD Practitioner:

You will be closer to satisfying the profession's craving for many years – to get closer to 'the business'. Once the organisation's competencies have been properly defined, you will then be able to structure all of your activity to meet your customers' real (not imagined) needs. Think of your function as selling a product or service. Without a real and thorough definition of a customer's needs, one can only 'best guess' the right solution, then attempt to 'hard sell' it to the customer. We all know what a hard sell feels like! Fully consultative selling, on the other hand, means that seller and buyer engage in full exploration of the real needs. They are both then committed to the jointly-agreed solution, resulting in win/win all round. A competency approach moves away from internal service provider selling, consulting or negotiating, to a joint problem-solving approach.

The need for HR/HRD to get closer to the business is illustrated in the following case.

In one organisation we worked with, the Personnel and Training function had invested heavily in fees and resources to overhaul completely and update their Management Development Programme. They had proudly presented their fully-integrated schedule of training events, together with timetables to capture – over time – the entire management cadre of over 700 people. Instead of receiving the anticipated congratulations and sign-off, a note arrived from the Deputy Chief Executive, asking one simple question: "What are we developing these people FOR?"

He took the view that, in a stagnant market where cost containment was the issue, he needed to be convinced there would be business development benefits on 'the bottom line', as well as any personal development for individuals. The credibility of Personnel and Training was further damaged, when they discovered – only after asking the right questions – that up to a third of the 700 managers might lose their jobs within 2 years.

The Personnel and Training function realised that a completely different approach was required, not just to regain their credibility, but perhaps even to retain their existence.

They rapidly developed some long-overdue consultancy skills among their people, then embarked on a competency-based approach to all of their activities (not just the ill-fated – and never resurrected – Management Development Programme).

This leads on to a vital issue – that of ownership. Whilst an HR/HRD function may often, quite rightly, be the instigator of work to define the agreed competencies in an organisation, the ownership must transfer at the earliest opportunity to the business itself.

Business managers must drive the quest for accurate definition, even if facilitated by HR/HRD. Competencies-based activity must always be perceived as relevant and valuable to line managers, or ownership may swing back to where it does not belong and may die a slow death. This requires continuous development of HR/HRD internal consultancy skills (and realistically, sometimes some selling!).

Why Have They Become So Popular?

One of the driving forces behind the need to develop a clear understanding of competencies is to enable organisations to understand and better measure performance. Once the performance drivers are clearly understood, it becomes possible to increase the prospects for high performance, throughout the business.

The starting point for understanding performance in any organisation is to gain agreement on what constitutes high performance and to put in place a framework which all can understand and acknowledge as the key drivers of high performance. Competencies have been described as the glue which binds an organisation together, taking a holistic look at the people, purpose, processes and performance.

In Chapter 4, Analysing Competencies for Your Organisation, we have detailed scenarios around a number of key performance indicators in an organisation. The recognition that competencies can improve effectiveness in such areas as:

•   recruitment and selection

•   retaining new entrants

•   assessing potential

•   assessing performance

•   training and development

•   succession planning

has caused organisations to embrace the concept and apply the competency approach.

Clearly defined competencies can also make a difference when considering flatter structures, increasing empowerment, downsizing and other organisational changes. Special considerations for these and others are contained in

•   Chapter 6 (Using Competencies)

•   Chapter 7 (The Pitfalls and Potential Barriers in Using Competencies) and in

•   Chapter 8 (A Practical Plan for Implementation).

Nationally, there has been increasing recognition of the need for a highly-skilled workforce, flexible and mobile, for overall prosperity. This has led to a plethora of nationally-funded training initiatives, many geared towards common evidence of an individual's capabilities through competencies. The Management Charter Initiative (MCI) is an example.

The world is becoming ever more competitive. Some of our work is in the Asia-Pacific Region, where the so-called 'tiger economies' – according to some – are having an easy time achieving growth and competitive edge, largely through cheap labour. This is not so. There is a clear focus on performance and effectiveness, coupled with a hunger for increased knowledge and skills at national, corporate and individual levels. We are currently engaged in a number of competency-based projects in that region.

The recognition of prospects for increased competitive advantage is driving forward further progress. No country, or organisation, can afford to ignore the quest for peak performance.

How Do They Work? How Can They Be Applied in the Workplace?

These two questions address the whole *raison d'être* for this report. Too many organisations have been deterred from adopting the competency approach, afraid of getting lost in the jargon, fearing horrific set-up costs, concerned that focus might be drawn away from the day-to-day business of actually doing business and for a myriad of other reasons. Most of these could be placed under a heading 'fear of the unknown'.

The reality is usually that:

- uncomfortable jargon masks some deceptively simple concepts

- set-up costs need not be high, depending on the degree of internal job analysis required

- if preferred, the competency approach can be phased in as a series of reviews: of recruitment procedures, of appraisal systems, of training provision, etc.

- the competency approach actually focuses right down on the real issues of business performance, probably in sharper focus than ever before

- as with many new initiatives, once business managers grasp the idea of competencies, they become complete converts, because the introduction makes it so much easier to manage performance and performers.

If in doubt, call the authors direct. First consultations always come free!

What Value Can They Add?

In Chapter 4, Analysing Competencies for Your Organisation, we list the potential stimuli in organisations, where a competency approach could add value through a more cohesive and focused strategy for people issues.

In Chapter 6, Using Competencies, we examine their use in at least six practical applications. Again, the aim is added value.

Competencies are a way forward, not the end. They can add real value to any organisation:

- as an aid to recruiting, managing and developing the right people, for the right jobs, in the right way

- by sharpening the focus on understanding the factors that cause real high performance

- by allowing the organisation to replicate (not clone) high performers throughout the business, through structured development.

Competencies provide a structured way of looking at people and jobs. They have the potential to become one of the most important tools in the kit labelled 'organisational performance'. They will not replace all the other tools, but should provide a structured framework to weld together the people, purpose, processes and performance.

2   A framework for understanding skills

Most progressive organisations have always been concerned to improve the quality and application of the skills of all employees. This is particularly true when considering the nature of management and the application of management skills. In a time of turbulent change, when organisations recognise that the demands which are being made on people to perform better are increasing all of the time, it becomes even more important.

As we said in Chapter 1 of this report, one of the driving forces behind the need to develop a clear understanding of competencies is to enable organisations to understand and better measure performance.

The starting point for understanding performance in any organisation is to gain agreement on what constitutes high performance and to put in place a framework which all can understand and acknowledge as the key driver of high performance.

We have taken as our example a discussion about management skills but the process we describe can be easily adapted to identifying and applying competencies to any group of employees.

Understanding Management Skills

The difficulty for most organisations is to be able to identify and isolate the characteristics of the high performing manager. In other words, what is high performance? What contributes to it and what makes it different? In many organisations, unfortunately, it is not only difficult to identify what constitutes high performance, there are often contradictory messages being sent: on the one hand, messages which are designed to encourage a more open, consultative style, and on the other, performance reward systems which focus entirely on getting the job done at all costs.

It is easy to see why many of these difficulties have arisen. It is only in recent years that people have been attempting to understand what 'good' management and therefore what constitutes a 'good' manager means. This may seem a somewhat surprising statement to make but just think about your own organisation and ask yourself how a range of managers in different parts of the business assess performance. Evidence from research conducted in connection with performance appraisal indicates that an ongoing problem with appraisal is that it is perceived by many employees as being too subjective and too dependent on the whim of an individual manager.

Different managers are perceived as having different expectations and applying widely differing standards, suggesting that managers have different views about what constitutes high performance.

The truth is that few organisations have attempted to define in any clear way what a high performing manager does. Different people use different models and different assessments of performance. Most of these will be subjective and based on the personal style and experience of the person making the judgement.

Management skills need to be explored within the context of what managers actually do and in most organisations this encompasses a very wide range of activities.

Many of these activities, although important, may be approached in what appears to be a fragmented way, with time being spent on them in short bursts rather than in a carefully planned, systematic way. Contrary to what many people would like to think, the average manager does not engage in very much planning, relies on instinct, albeit seasoned by experience, for most decision making and learns to play a wide range of roles.

Much of a manager's job is inevitably reactive, responding to the needs of his/her manager, customers, direct reports and peers, to name but a few. The amount of time spent reacting appropriately, as opposed to just reacting, to any and all demands may well be a key element in determining the effectiveness of the manager.

This diversity in what a manager's job is actually about makes it difficult, but perhaps more important, for organisations to ensure that they have a clear understanding of what constitutes high performance.

Understanding what managers do is the first step in differentiating the skills which high, average and low performing managers apply in doing their jobs. It provides a basis for setting standards of performance for key tasks, for developing plans for training and development and provides valuable information on which performance can be appraised. In addition, of course, it provides a basis for organisations to be able to start the process of establishing what the key competencies for their managers should be.

Developing a set of competencies which are agreed throughout the organisation is often a way through which organisations can take a more strategic approach to the whole process of career management. Most organisations find it helpful to start the process of developing competencies by first putting together a framework within which the competencies can be applied.

What is a Framework?

Put simply, a framework of competence is a number of key descriptors written in broad terms, providing a framework within which competencies can be derived and described. An example of such a framework could be:

1.   Managing yourself

2.   Managing your team

3.   Managing performance

4.   People development

5.   Trust and empowerment

6.   Purpose, goals and commitment

7.   You and your customers.

Some organisations use a framework such as the above, while others opt for a simple three or four step framework such as:

1.   Managing self

2.   Managing the task

3.   Managing people

or

1.   Business acumen

2.   Open thinking

3.   Personal style

4.   Impact on others.

Frameworks are sometimes referred to as core competencies or clusters, out of which the specific organisational competencies are derived. Within the context of a framework the actual number of competencies defined varies between organisations and ranges between 5 or 6 at the lower end, up to in excess of 40 at the higher end.

Having too many competencies can lead to repetition and confusion while having too few can mean that you are not covering a wide enough range of key management tasks. Most organisations opt for a framework covering 5 or 6 key areas of management, with each element within the framework including up to a further 4 or 5 competencies, giving a total of 20 to 25 competencies. Our experience suggests that, while without wanting to be unduly restrictive, it is much better to work hard at defining and agreeing a smaller number, rather than a larger number.

A framework covering 5 or 6 key areas of management activity, out of which flow up to 20 competencies, is likely to be more user friendly and manageable than a larger number.

Identifying the Competencies

When identifying the list of competencies most appropriate for your organisation it is important to obtain agreement, not just about the words to be used, but about what the words mean. In other words when we say, for example, that a personal competence for a manager will be 'Personal organisation' we need to provide a description of what this means. This might be stated as follows:

Personal organisation

- the ability to manage time effectively

- focus of effort consistently applied to where most impact will be achieved

- use of resources is structured so as to enhance personal effectiveness

Without some form of description of what the words mean, too much can be left to personal interpretation, with the danger that some words will be interpreted and applied differently by different people.

A Sample List of Management Competencies

An example of a possible list of management competencies, with suggested descriptors, for use as a starting point in reaching agreement about those most appropriate to your organisation could include the following:

Business awareness

- keeps in touch with current thinking and uses corporate strategy and business need to determine personal action

- has clear goals which focus on outputs and results

- has a wide spread of contacts throughout the business and uses them to stay in touch with developments and requirements across the business

Challenges assumptions

- is not afraid to challenge opinions and traditions

- does not settle for standard solutions

- seeks opportunities for continuous improvement

Personal organisation

- the ability to manage time effectively

- focus of effort consistently applied to where most impact will be achieved

- use of resources is structured so as to enhance personal effectiveness

Tolerance of stress

- the ability to live with ambiguity and uncertainty

- the ability to recover from setbacks and disappointments

- the capacity to cope with stressful situations and operate successfully when under pressure

- the ability to control personal feelings and emotions when under pressure

Self motivation

- sets personal goals and targets

- sets and achieves high personal standards of performance

- self starter, does not need constant supervision

Setting priorities

- is able to identify and concentrate most effort on critical tasks

- is able to balance the amount of attention given to important and urgent issues

- is able to balance personal needs and goals with the demands and requirements of others (e.g. customers, direct reports, other colleagues, own manager and suppliers, etc.) while optimising results

Confidence

- demonstrates personal conviction and belief in own ability, without this being seen as over confidence or arrogance

- acts confidently even when faced with uncertainty

- willing to back own judgement when taking calculated risks

- self belief in own ability and potential to succeed

Self development

- reflects on and learns from experience

- seeks out training and development opportunities

- demonstrates a willingness to engage in new experiences

- is capable of identifying personal strengths and weaknesses

- seeks feedback in an effort to improve personal skills

- can accurately assess own level of performance

Managing the team

- is able to develop group cohesion and commitment to team values

- provides regular feedback on the achievement of team goals

- openly celebrates team success

- is able to optimise the talent, expertise and experience of team members

- is approachable, supportive and helpful to team members

Leadership

- is capable of setting direction and standards for others

- can inspire and enthuse others to give of their best

- can positively influence the behaviour of others through personal example

- takes responsibility for others as the situation demands

Integrity

- is seen to be honest and fair in dealings with others

- can deal responsibly with confidential and sensitive information

- is able to win the trust of others

- does not take personal advantage of authority or position

Teamworking

- recognises the contribution of others

- involves others in achievement and success

- harmonises team relationships

- recognises the needs and feelings of others

- ensures effective communication and conflict resolution within the team

Management style

- is capable of using a wide range of management behaviours

- can diagnose and use the most appropriate management style

- gains commitment from people in different parts of the organisation

Open minded

- demonstrates a capacity to listen and understand alternative viewpoints and opinions

- can assess issues and people on their merits

- refrains from jumping to conclusions too quickly

- is capable of considering a range of options before taking a decision

Ability to influence

- is able to persuade others to accept alternative views

- convinces others through the power of logic and reasoning, not authority

- can resolve differences and conflicts between others through seeking and identifying common ground

Developing others

- looks for ways to develop team members in their roles and beyond

- regularly reviews the development needs of team members against their objectives and ensures that appropriate training is delivered effectively

- provides regular feedback on the achievement of personal and team goals

- is an effective coach

Face-to-face communication

- can present information clearly and logically to individuals and groups

- willingly shares information

- regularly informs and briefs team members and colleagues about developments within the business

- is able to involve others in meetings and discussions through the effective use of questions and good listening skills

Interpersonal skills

- builds rapport and is able to establish productive relationships with others

- can adopt a personal style appropriate to the individual and/or situation

- mixes easily and comfortably with a wide variety of people

- makes a positive impact on others in both formal and informal situations

Ability to motivate

- generates commitment and effort from others

- creates a climate which encourages the involvement and commitment of others

- creates an enthusiastic working environment in which team members are encouraged to make a full contribution

- is able to get the best out of people through understanding and responding to their aspirations and needs

Openness

- freely shares ideas, thoughts and feelings with others

- consults and involves others in developing plans and strategies for future action

- creates an atmosphere where people feel well informed and want to contribute

Problem solving

- deals promptly with difficulties and problems

- chooses the most appropriate solutions to problems

- identifies why targets and plans are not being achieved

- can gather and process relevant information systematically

Conceptual ability

- identifies original and innovative approaches and solutions to situations and challenges

- can create frameworks or models which help to make sense of complex issues

- can assess and balance a range of factors when making decisions

- can identify alternative approaches when solving problems

- cuts through detail to get to the core of an issue

Handling complexity

- is able to focus on the essentials in a given situation

- can identify the important elements in complex or confused situations

- listens to all sides before making a decision

Results orientation

- demonstrates a high personal motivation to achieve

- regularly achieves high performance levels

- actively strives to promote the development of new business opportunities

- ensures that personal effort is focused on priorities

- is able to make things happen

- takes corrective action with a sense of urgency

Competitive

- shows a desire to be the best

- inspires a winning approach

- constantly looks for ways to improve performance

Change orientation

- enjoys variety

- accepts and copes positively with a changing environment

- recognises change as an opportunity not as a threat

- responds positively to new demands and requirements

Initiative

- takes personal responsibility for tackling difficult situations

- seeks to shape or control events rather than react to them

- looks for new ways of doing things

- accepts responsibility readily and easily

- prefers to anticipate events rather than react to them

Customer concern

- demonstrates a clear commitment to achieving high standards of customer service

- listens to customers and seeks to identify and meet customer needs

- responds quickly to customers' expectations

- is always aware of the customer

- measures customer satisfaction

Quality

- utilises resources fully

- delivers a quality product or service

- assesses events in terms of value for money

- is aware of achieving the most appropriate balance between inputs and outputs

It is important to understand that this list should only be used as a starting point; it is not a recommended list of competencies. It is intended as an example of how an organisation could start the process of identifying appropriate management competencies.

Conducting a Management Competency Survey

There are a number of methods of analysis which organisations use to establish competencies and these are considered in detail in Chapter 5 of this report. At this stage it is useful to consider one approach which can be used in establishing specific competencies but which can also be used to derive a framework for management competence as it applies to the organisation.

A questionnaire should be developed and sent to each member of the senior team. Each organisation needs to define for themselves who should be included in this group, but it should include a representative selection of senior managers. The questionnaire will seek the views of managers on the competencies they believe will contribute to success in the company in the next few years.

The questionnaire should include a range of competencies within a suggested framework – the above or a similar list of competencies can be used as a starting point. Respondents to the survey are asked to comment on the framework and competencies, suggesting changes and or additions as appropriate. They should be asked to choose and rank an agreed number of competencies from the list provided.

Following completion and analysis of the questionnaire, structured interviews should be conducted with a number of the key senior managers in order to probe and build on the information obtained from the questionnaire. Once the interviews have been completed and the results analysed an initial framework and set of competencies can be prepared.

The next step is to test the framework and the competencies by involving a wider range of managers. This can be done by circulating a revised and updated questionnaire to a selected number of managers to seek their views on the framework and competencies as defined so far. Following this, once again it will be useful to interview a number of managers to probe and build on the information gained.

Once this stage has been completed the framework and list of agreed competencies can be tested by applying them to role models, through interviews and critical incident techniques, to firm up and test the viability.

Once the whole process has been completed a final list of competencies within an agreed framework can be agreed and approved for use within the organisation.

Rather than relying only on the survey method we recommend that organisations consider applying alternative methods of analysis in order to test the validity of the competencies which have been identified. A selection of alternative methods is outlined in Chapter 5 of this report.

Standards of Performance

It is only possible to assess how effective an individual is at doing their job if the expected outcomes of the job are clearly defined and communicated to the job holder. If they are to be truly effective, every individual needs to know, not only what they are expected to do, but what the outcomes of this should be and how success will be measured. In essence, what the expected outcomes of each job are should be clearly known by each job holder. This is often done by setting objectives for particular parts of an individual job and it is useful to think of performance standards as the standing objectives of a job. Those are the outcomes from a job which are to be achieved on a regular basis. They can sometimes be stated in quantitative terms which are readily measurable, but equally they can be stated in a qualitative way covering aspects of a job which may be less easy to measure.

Once these expected outcomes, or standards of performance, are known, it is possible to compare and measure how well people are performing. The most common measurement of standards of performance in organisations is a rating scale which is often applied to the performance of an individual at the annual appraisal. But standards of performance need to be much more visible, and seen to be achieved on a more regular basis than just through the annual appraisal.

An important distinction between standards of performance and competencies is that standards of performance apply to the characteristics of a job, while competencies apply to the ability of an individual to do that job. We can think of competencies as 'what does someone need to be good at, to be good at their job?'

Applying Competencies to Standards of Performance

A valuable use of competencies is applying them to help us to understand what an individual needs to be able to do, in order to achieve a particular standard of performance.

Assuming that the standard of performance for a particular task has been identified, the following process can be used in identifying and applying appropriate competencies:

* Analyse the nature of the task leading to the stated standard of performance.

* Identify the nature of the skills, knowledge, behaviour and attitude required to complete the task successfully to the standard required.

Take for example a bank teller serving a customer at the bank counter. The standard of performance is:

* Each customer will be greeted with a smile and a spoken good morning/afternoon. On accurate completion of the transaction, the teller will thank the customer using the customer's name and an appropriate closing remark such as good morning/afternoon.

Having identified what is required it now becomes possible to agree what competencies will be needed to achieve this standard of performance. These can be broken down as follows:

* Knowledge – the teller must be aware of the standard of performance required, where, within the various documents which may be presented, to find the customer's name and the skills required to complete a range of transactions.

* Behaviour – the teller must behave in a positive, friendly way, smiling and engaging eye contact with the customer and by taking the initiative by greeting the customer at the outset and at the end of the transaction.

* Attitude – the attitude displayed by the teller must be sincere, underpinned by a genuine desire to help.

These competencies, it should be noted, are very specific and related to a particular part of a particular job. Most competencies, such as the examples of management competencies shown above, will be more general and will therefore have a more general application. How general the application should be will depend on the requirements of the organisation. A more specific definition of a competency or set of competencies allows for more effective measurement of performance. But perhaps the time and effort required to achieve this can only be justified where there are a large number of similar jobs which are crucial to the success of the organisation.

Can Competencies be Applied to All Jobs?

Competencies can, of course, be applied to all of the jobs in an organisation; the only restriction is the amount of time and effort required to achieve this, set against the value which it would deliver. In an organisation where there are a lot of similar jobs, such as the example of the bank teller, the time and effort required to identify the key competencies for the job will be time and effort well spent. In many other cases a more generic approach to competencies may be more appropriate.

3   The competency approach

The time and effort which an organisation has to devote to developing competencies demands that a good return on the resource investment is achieved. Managers need to feel that time spent on identifying competencies will be time well spent. In Chapter 6 of this report we consider the practical application and use of competencies in a number of ways; in this chapter we propose to outline what can, in broad terms, be described as the competency approach. This is about considering how the development of competencies can provide added value and assist an organisation to take a consistent view about how they approach issues such as:

-       job profiling and job descriptions

-       training and development

-       performance review.

All three areas can be greatly affected by the development and implementation of competencies.

Competency Based Job Profiles and Descriptions

A job description can be described as a statement about the purpose, scope, tasks and responsibilities which constitute a particular job. The description can be further developed by including an indication of the key result areas and accountabilities which attach to the job. This approach to understanding particular jobs is focused very much on what the job consists of; it says little or nothing, except by implication, about the qualities required by the job holder. Traditionally this type of job description would be supported by a personnel specification which would describe the qualities, personal characteristics, knowledge and skills required by the person doing the job.

Unfortunately, in many organisations job descriptions have tended to fall into disuse, being updated only during job evaluation exercises and seldom being used in a positive way to help people do their jobs more effectively. In some organisations they are brought out and dusted off when it is necessary to find a replacement or additional member of staff. The problem, very often, is that they are tied to an idea of the job which is out of date and not related to what the job holder actually does.

A criticism of this approach is that it is static. Job descriptions like this are out of date by the time they are written. Managers and job holders make little effort to keep them up to date and generally they provide line managers with little by way of added value.

When asked, however, if they need to understand the jobs of their people the majority of managers say that yes of course, they need to understand what their people are doing. They need to be able to assess performance and to identify training needs and the job holder needs to be able to develop an understanding of the priorities of the job and the most important outputs. So some way of describing the job is essential.

They also need to have some understanding of the qualities of the type of people who will be best suited to doing a particular job. This is where the whole idea of competencies can add real value, as each of these requirements can be covered by a detailed analysis and understanding of the competencies required by particular job holders.

Job Profiles

Once competencies have been identified, many organisations have found it useful to move away from the traditional idea of job descriptions and have instead developed job profiles. A job profile is a single document which combines each of the elements of the traditional job description and personnel specification.

Developing a job profile starts with applying specific competencies to each key job. In the majority of organisations all of the general competencies which they have identified will not apply to all of the jobs. Where, for example, there are 20 competencies identified it may be that for some jobs only 10, or even less, will be considered essential.

A job profile will identify which of the competencies apply in the case of the particular job under consideration. The profile will describe each competency and the associated behaviours, outlining how the job holder has to behave for effective performance in the job.

The other key element in a job profile is job related information, including the job title, a summary of the role and responsibilities and an indication of the accountabilities. Where job profiles have been developed they have been found to be a source of valuable information for managers, in particular for recruitment and selection, for the identification of training needs and for acting as a basis for assessing performance.

Competency Based Training and Development

Competency based training is essentially about taking the framework and set of competencies which the organisation has developed and using this to structure the training provision to ensure that it matches the identified competencies.

Traditionally, organisations have identified training needs as a result of a two-pronged process, considering first the needs of the organisation and then comparing this with the skills of individuals and groups of employees. This worked by reviewing the environment in which the organisation was operating, looking at the market needs, identifying any major changes driving a need for a new response from the organisation in terms of product or skill, or both. It required training and development professionals to be constantly aware of the changing needs of the organisation in order that they could prepare timely training interventions designed to meet new and sometimes ever changing demands.

Having identified a new demand, the next stage was to assess the skill, knowledge and attitude of the employees who would be expected to respond to meeting the demand. This might be in terms of a change of operating practice, such as the introduction of a new computer system, or in terms of demand for a new service. An example which comes to mind is the way the role of service providers in retail financial services has changed in recent years.

In the not too distant past, a teller working in a retail financial services organisation was expected to serve customers courteously and efficiently, to deal with queries which the customers raised and to make sure that each individual remained a satisfied customer. In recent years the role of the teller has changed considerably; they are still expected to do all of the above, but they are also expected to take an active role in selling the additional products and services which the organisation has to offer. For many, effectiveness is now more about how many additional products they sell than how well they serve customers. This change has had major implications for the training and development of this group of employees.

Taking the two elements together, the change in the needs of the organisation and the change in skills required by employees indicates a need for additional training for this group of employees. These two elements are a useful way of considering the identification of training needs, representing as they do the needs of the organisation to meet the demand for change and the need for new skills in relation to a particular group of employees.

This particular change took place over a number of years and was not, as is the case with some changes, suddenly sprung on the training and development professional specialists. In an organisation which had been working on developing competencies the changing skill needs of tellers would have been identified as part of the process and that could have been built into the competencies for tellers.

The analysis of training need is about:

1.   Identifying current and, where possible, future organisational need for particular skills, knowledge and behaviours

2.   Assessing the current level to which the employees or group of employees perform in relation to these skills, knowledge and behaviours

3.   Identifying gaps which may exist.

Once the gaps have been identified, training plans can be prepared and put in place to bridge them.

With a competency based approach it becomes possible to identify more clearly and effectively the whole package of elements of personal knowledge and behaviour which will be required to perform particular jobs and sets of jobs to the highest standard. This enables the training and development professionals to identify training need more accurately in terms of organisational need. It also enables them to apply this more effectively to assessing the competencies of individual job holders and groups of job holders. This in turn should lead to a more effective and timely training response, better targeted and geared to meeting the real needs of both the individuals and the organisation.

How all of this is applied will differ from one organisation to another; however, what is clear is that once competencies have been identified, training can become more cost effective. The reasons driving this include:

•   training is perceived as being more relevant to meeting the needs of job holders

•   training is better targeted to meeting individual need

•   it becomes possible to demonstrate a clear link between the training provided and the stated competencies required for particular jobs

•   both trainers and trainees understand better what the training provision is seeking to achieve.

How training in relation to competencies can be applied is covered more fully in Chapter 6 of this report.

Competency Based Performance Review

Competency based performance review is essentially about how organisations use competencies to improve the way they assess and provide feedback in respect of an individual's performance.

The development and widespread communication of competencies and the associated behaviours equips both individuals and managers with a clear understanding of what is expected of them in their job. This enables the job holder and the manager to engage in constructive discussion about performance and development.

The performance standard required is more widely publicised and understood by all job holders and they can more readily conduct a personal review of their performance. Measuring their personal performance against a clearly defined set of competencies as outlined in their job profile becomes easier and more based on agreed standards. They can also assess more accurately any gaps which exist in the skills they require to do their job and make plans for development.

The manager can also conduct a more objective assessment of performance and training need against the same clearly identified expectations and competencies for each job holder.

Competencies allow the whole process of measuring performance to be more open and inclusive of all of the interested parties.

In some traditional approaches to appraisal, the assessment of performance is left too much to individual interpretation of some words and measures of performance. Because of the way competencies are developed and applied they are more generally acceptable to those to whom they apply. They are seen to have a high degree of direct relevance to the jobs which people do and are therefore more likely to be accepted as a valuable aid to measuring performance.

4 Analysing competencies for your organisation

All organisations need to focus on performance improvement. Ultimately, most improvement comes from maximising the potential of the organisation's people – as many Annual Reports quote: "...our most valuable asset."

There is no doubt that a universal understanding of competencies will help senior managers to better understand and measure performance. Yet, the potential within a competency approach is much wider than mere performance measurement. Before embarking on any research leading to recommendations, it is important to:

- understand the full potential for change, once competencies have been accurately identified;

- discuss the potential applications with senior management and other interested parties within the organisation;

- decide which activities should be based on a competency approach, including strategic priorities and timescales;

- draw up a (project) plan for the research, implementation and evaluation stages;

- ensure that the full plan achieves top-level approval and commitment.

These steps are vital, to put some boundaries around the work about to commence. A competency study, originally undertaken for the sole purpose of identifying and nurturing high-flyers, would almost certainly be inadequate to support recruitment and selection, for example.

It is most likely that a top-level decision to adopt a competency-based approach, will impact on more than one area of HR/HRD activity.

In a competitive environment, training can often begin as the focal point. True organisational effectiveness demands better-targeted training interventions, seen to have relevance and represent value for money when translated into bottom-line performance improvement. This can be a catalyst for change. Subsequent adoption of the outputs of competency studies, to drive activities not originally considered when those studies were undertaken, may result in damaging assumptions being made.

It is vital, then, to adopt a structured approach from the very start. The exercise should be managed and executed as one would any major project linked to organisational change. We have been called in to help organisations unravel multi-faceted competency projects which have lost sight of their original desired outcomes, have been ridiculously expensive in terms of internal resource commitments, and have also managed to alienate senior managers whose expectations have not been met. All of these unwanted and unpleasant outcomes could have been avoided with more time invested at the front end of the project, to ensure the degree of clarity necessary for success. In Chapter 7, we will expand on some of the pitfalls and potential barriers to success.

The studies to define competencies for the organisation will underpin all subsequent activity and application. This phase will be the most time-consuming and expensive, whether or not external consultants are engaged to assist in the work.

Before embarking on this phase, it is essential to be absolutely clear about:

•   what you are seeking to achieve, then

•   the objectives for your analysis.

We shall deal with each of these aspects, below.

What are you Seeking to Achieve?

The impetus for some work to define competencies may originate in HR, or come from a business manager. As we have said elsewhere, the sooner that ownership (not just sponsorship) can reside with 'the business', the better. Being clear about the purpose, outputs and expectations, as soon as possible after the initial impetus, will help to keep the whole project on track, until the implementation stage.

At this stage, it is important to:

•   detail the initial impetus for defining competencies;

•   consider other people-related activities in the organisation that might be improved by adopting a competency approach;

•   identify, brief, then gain the commitment of the highest possible decision-maker in the organisation;

- either individually or (preferably) all together, facilitate discussion with all appropriate decision-makers, around the potential uses of competencies. This discussion should centre on the:

    what / why / how / benefits;

- depending on the size of the above group, it may be possible to include the key line managers, or at least a representative sample, who will be responsible for making the competency approach work. Valuable input may be gained from this group. In any event, their potential power should not be dismissed and their needs, opinions and commitment should be sought early in the project.

The objectives of the above activity will have included:

1.   To gain high-level commitment to mounting a competencies project.

2.   To ensure all senior decision-makers understand the impact that a competencies approach might have on their area of the business, are provided with sufficient information around the options open to them, and then make decisions on which activities should be linked to competencies.

3.   To inform key line managers of the potential benefits to be gained from a competency-based approach, collect their issues and concerns, then gain their initial commitment to cooperate in the research phase.

It may be necessary at a later stage to define expectations and deliverables. Be cautious about agreeing to unrealistic timescales: many of the analysis methods take time to organise, identify the right subjects, gain their agreement to participate, etc. It may be all you can do to provide a date by which you will have fully defined the project, detailed the projected number of person-days involved, listed dependancies, and so on.

In Chapter 6, we will deal in detail with using competencies in organisations. Listed below are some of the organisational issues which might well benefit from a competency-based approach:

Organisational Change. Virtually all organisational change – downsizing, upsizing, flatter structures, privatisation, globalisation, growth, cultural change, shifts in product range or marketing mix, etc. – involves moving people into different jobs and roles, then ensuring that they perform well as soon as possible. For example:

- **Downsizing:** which employees should be retained? Which will perform best in the remaining, broader-scope jobs?

- **Upsizing:** which employees are more likely to be effective and successful in the new structure?

- **Flatter Structures:** which have the right competencies to lead and direct a wider span of control?

- **Privatisation:** which staff have the competencies to transform from bureaucrat to effective performer in a free, competitive environment?

- **Culture Change:** who will more readily adapt and thrive in the future culture?

and so on.

Poor Performance in Key Areas. If sales, production or quality are below par or the expected level, it may be necessary to recruit or promote people with the right competencies to succeed. Competency-based selection might well lead to a competitive edge.

High Staff Turnover/Early Leavers. Moving to competency-based recruitment and selection is likely to match people with jobs more effectively, resulting in quicker optimum performance and improved job satisfaction. Satisfied staff are less likely to leave and staff who assimilate and perform quickly do not have to be 'let go'. The benefits, in terms of reduced recruitment and training costs, are obvious. The overall working environment is also likely to improve, if more staff achieve a higher degree of job satisfaction.

Need for Succession Planning. The age profile of senior managers, moves towards earlier retirements or expected growth may all herald the need for succession planning activity. Past performance does not necessarily indicate future potential. Measurement against identified competencies is more likely to identify potential senior managers.

Drive Towards Improved Meritocracy and Equal Opportunity. Competency-based measurement, in recruitment and selection, does not discriminate against (or for) gender, race, age or educational background. Demographic changes, as well as legislation or internal policy change, may prompt the need for more balance. More objective recruitment and selection tactics and techniques make for more robust HR policies, open to close scrutiny.

Need For More (Cost-) Effective Training and Development. Training and Development that is closely linked to clearly-defined and agreed competencies is likely to:

- be recognised by trainees and their line managers as directly contributing to job performance (and, hence, organisational objectives);

- be actively supported by line managers, who recognise its relevance;

- shorten the time taken for new starters to reach the expected productivity and performance quality standards (this will also be improved by employing people with the right mix of competencies to do the job);

- more appropriately develop the managers of the future;

- be easier to justify, by cost/benefit analysis.

- achieve sponsorship and sign-off by senior management.

The examples above should provide a good basis for discussions with senior management. It will assist the research and implementation planning greatly, if you can prioritise the intended applications. The original impetus may no longer be top priority, once senior managers fully understand the potential uses of competencies throughout the organisation.

We suggest that you agree on a first-level prioritisation in a simple form, such as: 'Must Do/Ought To Do/Nice To Do'. An idea of expected time targets for each application would also be helpful. Armed with this information, you will then be better placed to recognise the strategic importance to your organisation, fully define the project, then be able to negotiate for additional internal or external resources, to bring the whole project in, on time.

This leads on to:

Setting Clear Objectives for Your Analysis

In Chapter 7, we will deal with the pitfalls and potential barriers. A primary danger lies in allowing a competency study to gain a life of its own, tying up people all over the organisation for varying lengths of time for no apparent reason, no perceived benefit.

A competency study that is driven by an expected need to downsize the organisation, or any unpleasant or unwelcome change, naturally needs to be handled very sensitively. Generally, though, success will come from:

- Clarity

- Communication

- Commitment

- Cooperation.

Clarity underpins the other three C's and it is at this stage in the process that it is vitally important to be very clear about:

- which activities in the organisation are to adopt a competency approach;

- which actual jobs need to be analysed;

- which can be considered generic;

- whether non-common job features need to be included;

- whether specialist or technical jobs need to be analysed;

- whether the analysis needs to produce results for different levels of performance within each job, for example:

  - high performers

  - average performers

  - new entrants and / or low performers.

The next chapter, 'Methods of Analysis', will need to be studied carefully before being too specific about your objectives for the competency analysis. You may decide it is uneconomic or impractical to carry out all the research required to be certain of the veracity of your studies. It is, however, important to be certain about what you want to achieve, before deciding how to achieve it. We therefore suggest a two-tiered approach to formulating your objectives for the analysis phase:

- first, carefully determine precise objectives based on the outputs you believe should be achieved from a well-executed analysis, then

- modify these objectives, once you have considered the time and resource implications in collecting the data, weighed against the ultimate value to your organisation and the risks attached to not getting it right.

An important issue to consider at this stage is whether to start from scratch and define organisation-specific competencies, or whether to use as a starting point lists of competencies defined by:

a)   another organisation, where there are perceived similarities, or

b)   an independent third party, such as the UK's Management Charter Initiative (MCI).

We have worked from several different starting points. Generally, we have found the most successful approach to be the creation of organisation-specific competencies, using our own and other independent groups' models as a checklist to ensure that no important areas are missed. The decision on whether to create a unique set for the organisation is usually made against an arbitrary budget, set in advance, for the work. We believe that an organisation should first determine what can be gained from adopting a competency approach, then decide how much it is worth to get it right. Relevance to the needs of the business is paramount, as is the overall value of the exercise.

Chapter 8 covers 'A Practical Plan for Implementation', speaking to all of the stages in the process. The need for attention to the overall purpose, intended applications, then clarity of objectives, cannot be stressed too highly.

When defining the objectives, consideration should also be given to potential evaluation techniques and measures of success. If time permits, serious thought should be applied to the practicality of introducing the exercise through a pilot group of strategically placed managers or employees. Selection of this group would ideally be based on the ease of measuring differences which can be directly attributed to a competency approach.

5   Methods of analysis

In Chapter 2 of this report we described how to conduct a management competency survey, one of the key methods which organisations use in analysing and identifying competencies. This chapter describes a range of other methods of analysis including:

- role-modelling

- critical-incident technique

- repertory grid

- competency analysis workshops

- surveys

- in-depth interviews

- benchmarking.

Role-Modelling

It is possible to identify a set of competencies for an organisation through role-modelling. As we said earlier, one way of looking at what competencies are is to ask the question, 'What does someone need to be good at, to be good at their job?' Looking at what people actually do through role-modelling can provide a lot of useful information about what people actually do when doing their job. Identifying what job holders do can provide valuable insights into establishing what are the most appropriate competencies for an organisation.

The way role-modelling works requires first that you identify appropriate role models and then study how they do their job.

Identifying Appropriate Role Models

In identifying role models it is useful to make some comparisons between people identified as high performers and others who appear to perform less well. Assuming that you want to identify the competencies displayed by effective managers in your organisation, the following process will enable you to do this.

- Ask a group of senior managers individually to identify a number of people in your target population who, in their opinion, fall into the following categories:

  - potential high flyers

  - solid middle range performers

  - below average performers.

- Compare the lists and identify those you propose to use as your role models. Once you have identified the group you plan to use, you will need to go back to the senior managers who nominated them, to gain as much information as possible about why each individual was nominated. You need to clarify how performance was assessed and what criteria did each manager use for placing each potential role model in a particular category. This process will give you a lot of useful insights about how senior management perceive performance and valuable information you can now start to use in building a picture of competence. To do this properly you will need to prepare a carefully structured interview plan.

- The next stage is to gather as much evidence about the performance of your target group as you can: reference to previous appraisals, attendance at assessment or development centres, any relevant information which will help to clarify or throw light on the performance of the people in your pilot group

- Once you have completed the above you will have gathered a lot of information about the people who make up the pilot group and will be ready to move on to meeting with them and observing them in action

- You can do this in a number of ways, through structured interviews with each individual; through using critical incident interviews (see below for a description of this technique); direct observation of them at work; the application of a 360 degree appraisal; simulated observed exercises and role plays at a development programme. We recommend a mixture of these techniques together with a short period spent shadowing each member of the pilot group in a number of typical work situations.

  The purpose of all of this activity is to identify what each of them does – do the perceived high flyers operate differently to the others? if so, in what ways? As the researcher you are trying to gain insight and understanding into what they are doing, in doing their job.

- Once all of your assessment activity has been completed, the analysis and comparison can be carried out. The outcome should be a clear identification of the behaviours, skills and knowledge demonstrated by each category of manager in the pilot group. From this combined information you should be able to identify what it is that the identified high performers do differently to the others in the pilot group.

- Having identified this information you can you use it to develop the framework and set of competencies. Of course, the information you have collected will not easily fall into clearly identified categories, and the perceived high performers will not do all of their tasks in the most effective way. Some perceived low performers will deliver better results than high performers on some categories of competence. You need to conduct a careful analysis of the results of your research if you are going to gain maximum benefit.

Making Sure Role-Modelling Works

As with all techniques there are advantages and disadvantages to role-modelling. Role-modelling can be time consuming and the results achieved can appear to be contradictory. Experience in a particular organisation where some research was carried out identified that many of the highest performing managers were those who did not follow the commonly accepted behavioural norms, being driven by the need for a change in culture. They managed their operation through a traditional command and control style of management. Inevitably this created a lot of concern about which behaviours really do drive high performance and, truth to tell, there is no easy answer. In this organisation they were able to accept that achieving a more open and inclusive culture would take a long time and that during this process some contradictions to expected outcomes were inevitable.

Using role models to identify competencies will almost certainly work best if the approach is used to test a framework and set of competencies which have already been identified and detailed. Once the competencies have been identified and before they are published it can be very valuable to test their validity and relevance through applying them to a number of role models using the approach described above.

A disadvantage of the technique is that it can be very time and resource consuming and many organisations refuse to use it for this reason. However, it should be said that it is an extremely valuable way of gathering a lot of useful information and deepening the understanding of what the proposed competencies mean to a range of people.

Critical-Incident Technique

Critical-incident technique is a means of gathering information about real life incidents and how the people involved have reacted to the event or incident. As a method of analysis it can be used in one-on-one interviews, with groups or for self report, written or recorded on audio or video. It does tend to be more effective when the researcher is face-to-face with the respondents alone or in a group as this allows the researcher to probe and ask follow up questions.

In competency analysis it is used essentially to gain an understanding of what worked and what didn't work in a number of situations.

Examples of critical incidents might include:

•   a confrontation with a colleague, a customer or a subordinate

•   an unforeseen but challenging incident such as a need to make an unprepared presentation

•   an encounter between two people from which one or both derive some learning

•   a meeting which results in some form of change, in systems or procedure or in behaviour or expectations.

A critical incident is generally an experience from which the individual/s involved derive some learning. It is used to help assess what constitutes good performance or poor performance by analysing real events. The process the researcher uses is as follows:

1.   Explain what a critical incident is, giving some examples, as above.

2.   Ask the group or interviewee to think back over the previous few weeks to see if they can recall any such event or similar situation.

3.   Ask them to describe the situation. Pose the following or similar questions:

         –   Tell me about the situation?

         –   How did you respond?

         –   How did others respond?

–   What happened as a result of this?

–   Tell me about some of the behaviours you and others used?

–   What would you say were the most effective behaviours and skills used?

–   What were the least effective behaviours and skills used?

4.   The probing continues until you have a full understanding of the situation.

5.   You then turn to the outcomes and explore how effective they were, linking back to the skills and behaviours identified, in an effort to pin down exactly what worked and what didn't. This allows the researcher to identify a set of preferred skills or behaviours which can now be tested.

6.   Having identified and understood the critical incident the researcher can use this to test how other people would respond if faced with a similar situation.

In competency analysis the critical incident would then be tested by interviewing a representative sample of managers to assess how each would act in the situation described.

Another way of using the technique is to design a number of realistic situations and explore with managers how they would respond. An example might be as follows.

As the researcher you want to explore a competency relating to personal standards so a sample situation might be:

•   'You have almost completed a difficult task, which has been worrying you for some time. You are now very close to your deadline and also have other imminent and pressing work and personal demands on your time. You ask a colleague to have a quick look at what you have done, expecting him/her to say "yes, that looks fine", in fact they say, "why didn't you include xxxx, I think it would add considerable merit to what you have done". You hadn't thought of xxxx and at this stage it will create considerable extra work and involve a lot more time.'

Allow the interviewee to consider the situation and then ask the following or similar questions designed to elicit information about the event or 'critical incident'.

- What action would you take next?

- Why?

- How would you describe your chosen behaviour?

- What would you expect the outcome to be?

- How would you expect your colleague to react?

- Would you describe your action as being most appropriate or as 'politically correct' (in the organisational sense), or both?

- If the action you would take was not 'politically correct' what action would be? Why didn't you take this action?

These, of course, are only sample questions, you need to devise your own in order to probe the situation you design and the competencies you are seeking to identify.

A disadvantage of the technique is that it can be time and resource consuming. It requires preparation and effort to get it right and many organisations decide that the effort is not worth the outcome. This, however, is not our view; we believe that it is important to test out the competencies you define in a way which mirrors real life. Using the critical-incident technique provide insight into management behaviour and competency which cannot be obtained by surveys and interviews.

Repertory Grid

Repertory grid is a form of interview during which the interviewer acts as a guide to the process rather than as a driver, which is often the more usual role of the interviewer. Interviewers almost always put something of themselves into the situation thereby acting as an influence, even if unintentionally, to the outcome. Repertory grid enables information to be gathered from an interview without this influence.

The process is based on Kelly's theory of personal construct. A personal construct is a way each individual views the world. A construct is personal in this way because it is the way an individual perceives it. Our constructs have a considerable influence on our behaviour and on the way we view the behaviour of others.

An interview using repertory grid begins with the selection of the topics for discussion, called 'elements'. When applying the approach to competencies the 'elements' under consideration would be the list of potential competencies. Each of these would be listed separately on a piece of card or paper as the interviewer would want to deal with each 'element' in turn.

The process is then as follows:

- The interviewer takes three elements at a time, from the set, places them on the table and asks the interviewee, 'which of these three is the odd one out, in terms of the qualities or attributes which an individual would need to perform it?'

- The interviewer then explores further to uncover more detailed definitions of the qualities identified, in terms of the behavioural characteristics. An example might be, the characteristic of 'self motivation' has been identified, so the interviewer could ask 'how would you know if an individual was demonstrating self motivation?, What sort of behaviours would we see?' The description the interviewee gives will represent their construct.

- What the interviewer is seeking to uncover is the constructs, which represent the personal view of the interviewee in relation to each element. It is through understanding the constructs that a picture can be built of what this potential competency means.

- The approach is repeated, using three elements each time, until all of the elements have been covered and the exercise is completed.

On completion the interviewer will have gathered a lot of information which will need to be considered and contrasted with information coming from other sources. We recommend that when using repertory grid for competency analysis it be used as part of a battery of techniques rather than as a stand alone technique.

Repertory grid works equally well in a one-on-one interview or in a small group. For an unskilled analyst, using repertory grid can be challenging and we recommend that before using this technique the analysts receive training and have an opportunity to practise the skills in situations which will not be included in the final competency analysis.

Competency Analysis Workshops

A popular way of defining competencies used by many organisations is through the use of competency analysis workshops. Selected groups of employees are invited to participate in a workshop, the purpose of which is to define a set of competencies which can be applied across the organisation.

In most cases more than one workshop would be held in order to canvass and compare a range of opinion. In planning for such a workshop it is advisable, but not essential to have previously developed a framework and list of potential competencies, such as the example shown in Chapter 2 of this report. The provision of a prepared framework and list of competencies helps to focus attention more quickly onto what is required, and enables quicker understanding of the process as it provides participants with an easy to understand frame of reference.

A disadvantage is that it can limit the scope of the discussion as it is often difficult for people to think outside of the framework and list which have been provided. Of course, in many cases the workshop would be seeking to test and validate the framework and competencies, not originate them. If this is the case it will be necessary to provide the framework and list.

Typical aims and objectives for a competency analysis workshop would be.

Workshop aim:

- to define a framework and set of competencies which can be applied to an agreed range of jobs in the organisation.

Workshop objectives:

Upon completion of the workshop participants will:

- understand what competencies are, and be equipped to apply them to a range of jobs

- have agreed a set of competencies which can be applied to jobs in the organisation

- have identified the specific behavioural descriptions which can be applied to each of the competencies.

A typical programme would start by outlining what competencies are, how they work and the benefits they bring to an organisation. Participants would then be invited to contribute their views and opinions.

Programme Outline

What are competencies?

- defining competencies

- how competencies work

- what value do they add?

- why introduce competencies?

- where do they fit?

How can we apply competencies to our organisation?

- an outline of the plan for the introduction of competencies

- what we will do

- how we will do it

- when we will do it

Agreeing a framework for competencies

- syndicate exercise during which participants define a framework for competencies which can be applied within the organisation

Report and review

- the whole group reviews the work of the syndicates and a recommended framework is prepared

Defining the competencies

- syndicate exercises during which participants identify and define the competencies and behavioural descriptions which can be applied in the organisation.

During this section of the workshop it will be helpful if the syndicates can work on different elements in the framework. After each group has completed a list together with the behavioural descriptions, these should be shared in plenary.

Once each element in the framework has been presented and discussed they should be re-considered in syndicate to take on board the views expressed in plenary. In doing this it is best to mix the groups, leaving some of the original participants in each group and adding some people who did not consider the particular topic before. This encourages participants to build on ideas rather than suffer the danger of a mental block caused by continuing concentration on work they have done previously.

Report and review

- the whole group reviews the work of the syndicates and a recommended set of competencies is prepared

After the workshop

After the workshop you will need to draw together all of the work into a usable format. It should then be presented to senior management for amendment and approval prior to publication and communication across the organisation.

Running a Successful Workshop

Using a competency analysis workshop to identify and define competencies can add a number of valuable benefits including:

- the final set of competencies will be more real and relevant as they have been defined by job holders

- line managers and employees rather than specialist and human resources staff have designed and are therefore more likely to own the framework and competencies

- as the competencies are owned by job holders they are much more likely to be used.

Success, however, is not necessarily guaranteed. There are many things which can go wrong, so careful planning and preparation is essential. The following checklist will help you to make sure that your workshop is a success.

Checklist for a Successful Competency Analysis Workshop

- **Clarify/agree terms of reference and objectives for the workshop**

  Make sure that the terms of reference and objectives for the workshop are agreed by all, in advance. Will the workshop be devising a framework and set of competencies, or will it recommend?

  Recommendation may be necessary as you might be running more than one workshop and will need to pull the results together; if this is the case someone will need to act as an editor. Recommendation may also be necessary as senior management may want the final decision about the framework and set of competencies. Both approaches are a valid way of working but you need to be clear what is intended before you start.

- **Think carefully about your choice of participant**

  Your choice of participant will be influenced by the terms of reference and objectives. However, you also need to consider the level of seniority and influence of each participant, the range and relevance of functions and departments from which they are drawn.

- **Make sure that workshop participants understand the terms of reference**

  At the start of the workshop the participants need to understand exactly what you are asking them to do, what the outcomes will be and what you will do with the outcomes.

- **Make sure that you understand what competencies are and how you propose to use them in the organisation**

  It is probable that some of the workshop participants will be sceptical about the whole concept of competencies. If you fail to convince them of the value and benefits the organisation will derive from this work, it is likely to undermine all you are seeking to do.

  You can overcome this by making sure you prepare thoroughly for the workshop and understand what competencies are and how you will apply them. Careful reading of this report will give you most of the information you need to know about competencies. Additional reading can be found in the bibliography. If you are still in doubt, seek the advice of professional colleagues or seek help from outside the organisation.

- **Make sure you get the organisation of the workshop right**

  This might sound obvious, but remember that you need the participants to feel good about the event right from the start. Poor or mismanaged organisation will create a bad impression and influence their perception of the value of the workshop.

- **Location and equipment**

    Give careful thought to the facilities and location of the workshop. A lot of time will be spent in syndicate exercises, so make sure that syndicate rooms are available. Three syndicates squashed into one small room work less effectively than one syndicate in one room.

    Make sure you have enough flipcharts; at least one for each syndicate will be required. An ample supply of flipchart pads, coloured pens, larger size 'Post It' notes, or similar methods of pulling together information quickly, will be needed.

Surveys

Conducting a survey is probably the most popular way of identifying the competencies most appropriate for any given organisation. In Chapter 2 of this report we outlined in detail how to conduct a management competency survey. As stated, the purpose of this survey is to establish a framework for management competencies and identify the most appropriate set of management competencies.

It is of course possible to adopt the same approach to establishing a wider range of competencies covering all jobs within an organisation. The process to follow would be very much the same with the necessary adaptations being made to the design of the questionnaire and the range of competencies to be included. The target population for receiving the questionnaire and for inclusion in the follow up interviews would also need to be extended as appropriate.

Given the nature of the competencies being identified in the example survey in Chapter 2 of this report we restricted the target population for inclusion in the survey and follow up interviews to members of the management team. In certain circumstances the following groups could also be involved in surveys to establish competencies.

Surveys of Customers

Competencies are designed to provide an insight into the all-round accumulated skills, knowledge, behaviour and attitude which individuals display in doing their job. It is therefore possible to argue that the people most likely to be affected by the way the job is performed – customers, both internal and external – should be involved in establishing, at least, some of the competencies.

To achieve this successfully we suggest the following process:

1.   Establish clearly the jobs you are seeking to identify competencies for.

2.   Identify the range of competencies you are seeking to enlist the help of customers in establishing. It is unlikely that you will want to establish the views of customers in identifying competencies across the whole of a job. You will probably want to restrict their involvement to those aspects of the job which have a direct impact on them. The more targeted the survey the more effective it is likely to be.

3.   Identify carefully the customers you are seeking to involve. Make sure that they can offer informed views on the areas of the job you are interested in.

4.   Make sure that you are asking each participant to compare like with like.

5.   Construct the questionnaire carefully, beware of ambiguities. Many questionnaires fall down because they are insufficiently clear. It is usually best to pilot the questionnaire in order to identify potential problems and get them ironed out before using it for real.

6.   Make sure you communicate clearly with participants what it is you are asking them to do; provide clear instructions for completion and return of the questionnaire.

7.   If you are planning to do follow up interviews, make sure you plan them equally carefully.

Customers provide valuable insight and information but as individuals they are prone to hold idiosyncratic views. It is therefore important to make sure that you do not base your competencies on the views of single individuals or an unrepresentative minority; great care is required in identifying the target population for a customer survey.

We advise that the same cautions should apply when dealing with internal customers as for external customers.

A Survey of Colleagues and Peers

Along with customers another group who will have a valuable contribution to make to the identification of competencies will be the colleagues and peers of a given group of employees. They will have insights and opinions which are likely to be well worth taking into account. The key, as with the customers, is to be clear about why you are involving them and what you are involving them in.

We recommend that the process as outlined above for conducting a survey of customers is followed with this group. Make sure you identify clearly which parts of the job you are asking them to comment on and ensure that you survey a representative group.

Other Groups to Involve

There are a further two groups that it can be useful to involve in analysing and identifying competencies, subordinates and the existing job holders themselves.

Subordinates or team members will have very clear views on the competencies required by their team leader. Experience suggests that they will have high expectations of the team leader and will often be looking for them to demonstrate a range of skills not identified by other groups. Contrary to the expectations of some managers a great many team members will not seek to use this as an opportunity to press for skills which may lead to an easy life for the subordinates. They are just as likely to press for competencies which will be demanding for the team leader to achieve and once achieved will be demanding of the team.

Some very interesting examples of how 'ordinary employees' behave when given freedom to make more decisions for themselves are contained in the book *Maverick* by Ricardo Semler (1993). They prove to be hard task masters on themselves as well as on their managers, suggesting that valuable insights could be obtained from this group in analysing and identifying management competencies.

Once again the involvement of this group needs to be carefully handled. Objectives must be clear, parameters identified and the process clearly communicated.

Few people, if any at all, would question the involvement of individuals in full participation in their own appraisal review via a process of self assessment. It seems reasonable therefore, to involve individuals in analysing and identifying the competencies required for doing their job.

Job holders bring a whole new set of insights into understanding what a job consists of. They have an understanding of elements of the job which are very often not obvious to others looking in from the outside. They understand the pitfalls to be avoided, those elements of the job they avoid doing and the opportunities for change which may exist.

They also have a real understanding of the competencies which are required and, providing they can be persuaded to respond in a fully open and honest way, they will be able to provide truly valuable insights into the competencies required.

360 Degree Analysis

Organisations are increasingly recognising the value of conducting 360 degree appraisals. We believe that the insights gained from this approach can be equally valuable when applied to the analysis and identification of competencies.

We would not suggest that there is a straight comparison; however, we would suggest that when analysing competencies an organisation has much to gain from casting the net wider than the obvious few.

The commitment and effort required in analysing and identifying competencies is always substantial. It is useful, however, to remind ourselves that we want to understand competencies because these are the skills, knowledge, behaviours and attitudes which lead to superior performance. The more accurate our analysis the more likely it will be that we achieve our objective of identifying what it is that drives superior performance.

In-Depth Interviews

It is true to say that whatever survey method you choose it can be greatly enhanced by following up a paper-based survey with a series of in-depth interviews. In-depth interviews allow for the information gained as a result of the survey to be validated. They enable the interviewer to probe for meaning and understanding behind the responses to questions.

Conducting an in-depth interview requires careful thought and preparation and we suggest the following process:

1.   Analyse the results of the survey carefully and identify those areas you believe it will be most valuable to follow up.

2.   Prepare a structure and set of questions for the interview.

3.   Inform the interviewee about what you are seeking to achieve out of the interview.

4.   Make sure you allow ample time for the interview; you may need to allow some time to explore areas you had not previously identified.

5.   Make sure you take ample notes or record the interview.

As part of your follow up to the interview you will need to allow ample time for the analysis of the information you have gathered. In-depth interviews provide a lot of information and it requires careful analysis to ensure that you get full benefit.

Benchmarking Competencies

Best Practice Benchmarking has been described as the constant search for best practice. It works by identifying organisations which deliver the best results in particular elements of business application, studying what they do and then adapting and applying what you have learned to your own organisation.

It is not simply about copying what other people have done and making it fit with what you do, but attempting to understand what they have done and seeing what, if anything, it is possible to apply in your own case.

There is a lot of information available generally about competencies and many organisations have already devoted a lot of energy to defining and applying competencies. It should not be difficult therefore to start drawing together information about what is already available and starting to identify other organisations who might share information with you. Contact with professional bodies and trade associations can often provide a lot of useful information.

We suggest the following approach for benchmarking:

1.   Clarify why you want to define competencies and how you will use them.

2.   Define your own framework and set of competencies to first draft stage.

3.   Identify organisations who you could benchmark with.

4.   Contact the organisations and find out if they are willing to share information about competencies with you.

5.   Establish a competency team/working party and make sure you involve them all in benchmarking. You will learn more from benchmarking through working in a small group of two or three than you will by doing it on your own.

6.   Arrange a meeting/s with the identified partners to share and explore what each other is doing.

7.   Conduct a thorough review of the information gained and feed this into the process you are using to define competencies.

8.   Maintain contact with your benchmarking partners for follow-up meetings and further sharing of information and experience.

Benchmarking can provide useful insight and information into the way you approach the identification and definition of competencies and in the longer term how you apply them. Our experience with benchmarking is that it is most likely to be successful when the sharing of information is two way. We do not recommend that you ask for information from other organisations without having something to share with them.

Finally, it is important to remember that the most appropriate competencies for your organisation are those which you and your colleagues identify as having the greatest application. Benchmarking will provide you with insight and information, it may answer a lot of questions and concerns. However, it should inform the work you are doing in identifying your competencies, not replace it.

A Word of Caution

Critics of competencies suggest that the nature of competencies is restricted to identifying what works now and what has worked in the past and that because of this competencies can trap the organisation in the past. Of course, this a danger which it is important to be aware of and avoid. No organisation would want to invest the time and effort into defining competencies if they were to be out of date a soon as they were designed. Every major initiative which an organisation engages in needs to build on the past but focus on the future. In a period when most organisations are experiencing turbulent change, they need to be constantly looking ahead and anticipating what is going to happen in the next period. This is as true when defining competencies as in so many other aspects of organisational life. Competencies can be a means of helping organisations to focus on the people needs of the future.

Our belief and experience is that it is possible to look ahead when analysing and identifying competencies. It is the focus and quality of the analysis which is important. It is in designing the analysis, whichever mix of methods you choose, which will decide how effective, relevant and lasting the outcome will be.

6 Using competencies

Once an organisation has identified and defined the key competencies which apply to key jobs, there are a number of uses to which the competencies can be put to help achieve improved organisational performance. In this chapter we will look at some of the more important of these, including:

- recruitment and selection

- training and development

- redeployment

- assessing potential

- succession planning

- managing performance.

In each case we will be seeking to provide a practical insight into how competencies can be used in improving performance and outputs.

A key use of competencies we decided not to cover in the report is that of pay. Many organisations use competencies as part of their total reward strategy, linking competencies to pay in relation to job grading, merit awards and multi-skilling. This area is one which we believe should be covered in a broader discussion of pay and reward strategies and as such should be covered in a report on pay strategies rather than in a report on competencies.

Recruitment and Selection

Selection in many organisations is more of a hit and miss affair than many would like to admit. The whole process of recruitment is costly and time consuming. The fact that it is time consuming may well be one of the reasons why so many fail to give it the attention it deserves, until it becomes urgent and forces itself up the list of priorities.

The process and procedure for recruitment is generally clear in the minds of most people:

1. identify a vacancy

2. review the need for a replacement

3.   update the job description

4.   update the personnel specification

5.   advertise

6.   interview

7.   assess

8.   appoint.

Unfortunately, in all too many cases stages two to four are ignored and the process moves directly from identifying the vacancy to advertising the job.

Competencies allow managers, even encourage them, to take a more considered approach to this process because they keep the notion of 'what type of person would be best for that job?' closer to the forefront of their mind.

Once competencies have been identified and defined they can be applied to the process of recruitment, helping to make this more efficient and relevant.

Most organisations, after agreeing the competencies most relevant to their needs, apply them to the recruitment process by preparing sets of job profiles. A job profile replaces the previously used job description and personnel specification and is constructed by reviewing the competencies which are identified as being most important for each job. In an average job this should work out as being no more than nine or ten critical competencies drawn from the total. In addition, the profile will give an indication of the level of competency to be achieved for the job holder to be seen to be demonstrating average effective performance and outstanding performance.

Job Advertising

Another application of competencies to the recruitment and selection process is in how an organisation presents itself in public through its recruitment advertising.

The development of job profiles enables the organisation to focus much more specifically on those competencies which are proven as being essential to effective job performance. This means that when writing job advertisements only those competencies which are essential need be included. Anyone who has trawled through many dozens of letters and application forms will recall the feeling of wishing that the description of the skills and qualities required for the job could have been better described in the advert. A clear understanding of the competencies required for a job enable more clearly focused adverts to be written, leading in turn to a response which is equally focused.

The same approach applies with equal force to the internally advertised job. Our experience suggests that many organisations create problems of raised expectations of internal job applicants because of a failure to communicate clearly. Often, too little information is available about the skills and qualities required for a particular job, leading to misunderstanding about the job requirements and the experience and qualities which will be required of applicants. Competencies and job profiles can help to overcome many of these difficulties and misconceptions.

Competency Based Interviews

The use of competency based interviews are becoming increasingly popular in a wide range of organisations. They can deliver a higher degree of objectivity in the selection process. And, because they are based on proven job requirements, they are found to be more effective in recruiting people who are more likely to be suited to the job more quickly.

It is important to understand that there is nothing magic or, for that matter, difficult in competency based interviewing. As we have seen earlier in this report, when defining competencies, a key output is to identify, under the description of each competency, how the competency describes the behaviour, skill and knowledge which will be applied by an individual job holder in doing the job.

Many organisations define competencies in behavioural terms stating that such and such a competency will be demonstrated by such and such behaviour. In Chapter 2, we gave as an example the competencies required by a bank teller in successfully doing part of the job. In this example we included a description of the behaviours described in doing the particular part of the job.

Assuming that a particular competence was considered to be an essential part of the job it becomes possible to test this element during the interview. This can be done by adopting a planned and structured approach to questioning and in more practical ways as well. Not only does this result in more effective interviewing, it also considerably increases the level of objectivity applied in the interview. It achieves this by ensuring that each candidate is asked the same questions and is assessed by using the same criteria for measurement.

This is not to suggest that recruitment interviews are generally less than objective and use different approaches to assessing candidates. It is to suggest, however, that in many interviews there is room for improvement.

Competency based interviews work by applying the following process:

- The job profile, describing the key competencies and descriptors is prepared.

- Interviewers are trained in how to assess competencies, in recognising behavioural indicators and in observation skills.

- A set of structured questions is prepared for use at each interview.

- Whenever possible some form of simple behavioural activity is built into the interview to provide some additional evidence which can be observed and assessed.

- A rating scale to help support and assess the questioning and observation used is prepared.

- An assessment form for completion at the end of each interview is prepared.

- The interviews are then conducted.

Some may complain that this appears to be creating a lot of extra work and effort. However, experience shows that time spent in preparation will deliver time saved and improved quality in the outcomes.

It is not difficult to see how this approach could be applied to interviewing a bank teller in relation to the behaviour and attitude described in the example given in Chapter 2 of this report.

The behaviour described could be assessed as part of the way the candidate presents himself/herself at start of the interview. Alternatively, a short role play could be constructed during which the interviewer asks the candidate to play the part of a teller, during which it will be possible to assess some of the key behaviours identified.

The attitude described could be tested by using a number of structured questions such as:

- How do you feel about shop assistants who take the initiative in greeting you when you are a customer?

- Tell us about a situation in which you have had to take the initiative in greeting someone.

    - How did you feel about this?

    - What did you do to help ensure success?

    - What have you learned from this experience?

- Describe a situation in which you have had to act as a service giver.

    - How did you feel about this?

    - What did you do to maintain a consistent approach when dealing with different people in this situation?

- Tell us about a situation when you offered to help someone.

    - What worked well in this situation?

    - What worked less well?

    - How did you feel about it?

The major difference between this type of approach and more traditional interview questioning is that the questions are specifically designed to explore with the candidate, the competencies required in the job. The interview is structured around the competencies and how the candidate can demonstrate prior experience in them.

The benefits we get from applying competencies to recruitment and selection can be summarised as follows:

- an agreed set of standards leading to more objective assessment

- job analysis which concentrates on what people do in order to do the job well

- job profiles which help a wide range of people to understand more fully the job requirements

- interviewers who are trained in assessment techniques

- interviewers who will use the same basis for selection in each interview

- better targeted and written job advertisements

- recruits who are better suited to the job and therefore more likely to stay.

Training and Development

The majority of organisations who use competencies use them in some way as part of the training and (management) development process. Competencies are used as a way of helping to ensure that each individual accepts a greater degree of personal responsibility for their own learning and development, rather than it being the responsibility of management. This fits closely with the view, which most professional trainers now subscribe to, that each individual should take primary responsibility for their own development. Of course, the organisation needs to put in place the means to support and encourage this approach to development, but ownership is firmly with the individual.

Once competencies have been clarified, individuals can more readily understand what they need to know and what they need to do in order to be good at their job. This means that training and development can be designed to meet the identified training needs of individuals rather than offering more generalised training solutions.

Competency Workshops

The starting point for training activity after the identification and development of competencies in many organisations has been to provide workshops for all groups of employees and individuals to whom the competencies apply. This has usually been as part of a major communications programme to ensure that everyone understands what competencies are about, how they work and how they will impact on identified groups and individuals.

In Chapter 5 of this report we provided details of a Competency Analysis Workshop. This workshop was held to assist with the identification and definition of competencies. As a part of the introduction of competencies across the business many organisations have found it helpful to develop and run a workshop, to inform and involve all employees in understanding competencies and how they will be applied.

A competency workshop requires a lot of careful planning and preparation. It will have only one chance to work, so it will be important to plan well in order to get it right.

To make it successful requires:

- clarity of aim and objectives

- confidence and clarity about the competencies being communicated

- clear plans for future action about the application and expectations for the competency programme

- what happens with competencies after the workshop?

- buy-in from top management.

A typical competency workshop would cover:

Workshop objectives

Upon completion of the workshop participants will:

- understand what competencies are

- understand our competencies, how our competencies have been defined and how they will be applied in the organisation

- be able to identify which competencies and supporting behaviours apply in their own job

- have started to assess their own level of competence in key areas and to build a personal development plan for further development.

Programme Outline

What are competencies?

- defining competencies

- how competencies work

- what value do they add?

- why introduce competencies?

- where do they fit?

How were our competencies defined?

- how competencies were defined

- who was involved

- what we are seeking to achieve

How will competencies be applied in our organisation?

- an outline of the plan for the introduction of competencies

- what we will do

- how we will do it

- when we plan to do it

An overview of our competencies

- this session will outline in detail the competencies in general and the specific competencies which will apply in the jobs of the people attending the workshop

- how our competencies fit together

Applying competencies in your job

- working in pairs or small groups participants will analyse each competency in relation to the accumulated skills, knowledge, behaviour and attitude required to achieve superior performance in their job and apply the competency

- the second part of this analysis will seek to identify performance gaps

Barriers to achieving competence

- participants will be invited to identify and explore barriers which may prevent the achievement of superior performance. Barriers may exist in the organisational climate or culture; in the way people interact with each other as managers, peers, customers; or there may be barriers within individuals themselves

- having explored potential barriers, they are asked to identify how they can be overcome

Planning for your development

- participants will be introduced to the idea of producing a Personal Development Plan, how it will work and what supports will be available

- how will the PDP be monitored?

Final Report and Personal Action Plan

After the Workshop

After the workshop all of the work must be drawn together so that people know what is expected of them. All participants need to understand what is expected of them now, what help is available for them to continue working on their PDP and where they can go to get this help. How and when will competencies be assessed in the future, will competency assessment be a part of the annual appraisal?

Other Training Requirements as a Result of Competency Definition and Application

Competencies have led to an increased need for training across a wider range of activity than a competency workshop, although it should be said that much of this has been demand led rather than provider led. In other words, more training is being provided but this is in response to demand from the managers and employees seeking to improve their skills and behaviours in order to more closely match the competencies which have been identified as being required for their job.

This has also meant that as well as improved provision for training in general, there has been a significant increase in the need for techniques such as coaching and mentoring, techniques which can help individuals to gain more immediate value from the time spent in development activity and for individuals to work on personal development plans.

Coaching and Mentoring

Coaching, as a management technique, has been around for a long time, but with the development of competencies the need for more effective coaching is highlighted. Individual employees are better informed about the specific competencies they need to develop if they are to do their job effectively. Training away from the job can help individuals develop many elements of their competency requirements. Other elements, however, often the most important, can only be developed and honed to the required standard through the deliberate application of coaching on the job.

This has placed an additional responsibility on managers and team leaders to develop their skills in coaching and learn to apply a coaching approach in their day-to-day activity.

We can think of coaching as any planned intervention by another person designed to improve the performance of an individual when performing a specific task. In these terms it is easy to see the importance which coaching has to supporting individuals in developing competencies, through the emphasis on improved performance in identified areas of activity.

Mentoring does not seek to assist the individual to develop specific skills but its relevance to competency development can be equally important. Mentoring helps individuals to make sense of their longer term learning needs and objectives, not so much which competencies an individual needs to develop now, but in helping the individual to think about what they want to do for the future and identifying which competencies will be required if they are going to achieve this.

Together, coaching and mentoring make the transfer of learning from a training environment more effective and relevant, they make it easier for individuals to apply learning, through making sense of where it fits. Individuals are looking for this application of learning, sometimes in the here and now and sometimes in thinking about and planning for the longer term. Either way, as a support to the application of competencies, coaching and mentoring are invaluable.

Personal Development Plans

We referred to personal development planning earlier and for any competency programme to be successful it is essential to provide all employees who are involved with the means of producing a Personal Development Plan (PDP).

A PDP enables each individual to:

*   understand the competencies required for achieving superior performance in their job

*   assess where they are now in relation to the competencies for their job

*   identify any performance gaps they may have to bridge to achieve superior performance

*   understand how to start bridging the gaps

*   be aware of what help is available

*   be able to monitor and keep a record of improved performance

*   call on their manager for help.

A typical PDP will include the following.

*   A copy of the job profile detailing the competencies required.

*   Any information about additional competencies which may be desirable but not essential.

*   Relevant information about standards of performance if any exists.

*   A method of assessing current level of performance against the competencies. This could be as simple as some form of self assessment supported by assessment by the manager. Alternatively it could involve much more sophisticated approaches, such as the results of psychometric assessments or the results and recommendations from a development centre. The purpose is to provide the individual with some indication of where they are starting from.

*   A method of analysing the assessment and applying the results to identifying performance gaps.

*   Assistance with the process for developing a plan for improving performance and achieving the competencies.

*   A space for outlining the objectives and detailed plan for achieving improved performance.

- Some form of time planner against which to record timescale objectives and plans for reviews of progress.

- Full details of any help which is available and where to find it.

Many organisations produce very elaborate folders and while this can help to indicate a level of importance and organisational commitment, it is not essential. The commitment which the individual and their manager makes each week, to developing and applying learning, together with the commitment of the organisation to the training need being met, is much more important. The application of coaching and mentoring, which an individual experiences each day, will be of greater importance than the best folder one could imagine. No folder can ever replace the personal interest and concern of a manager working with an individual to improve performance and skill.

Where Personal Development Plans have not been supported by the demonstrated commitment of managers to development they have, unfortunately, largely fallen into disuse.

Redeployment

Many organisations are faced with the need to consider redeployment for groups of employees as market forces drive the need for job changes. Employees need to demonstrate an ability and willingness to adopt a more flexible approach to working practices. When this happens employees are often fearful of the prospect of change and worried that they will not be able to learn the new skills required. This can lead to suspicion and a lack of trust in the employer. Of course, any situation which requires major change is always going to be fraught with difficulty and competencies will not provide an easy way out. They can, however, help to ease the difficulty.

The major problem in a situation like this is often the uncertainty created by the prospect of change. Competencies can help people understand more readily what will be required in the new environment. Where competencies have already been defined and published, concerned employees can be helped to understand what competencies will be required in the new jobs and what this means in terms of what they have already achieved and therefore have to offer. More importantly, they can greatly ease the process of assessment and selection for the positions which are available. Also, they can help to demonstrate that the process of assessment and selection is fair and above board.

The application of competencies to redeployment should work in a similar way to that applied in recruitment and selection, when selecting employees who are to be redeployed. This means that each individual is able to gain an understanding of what they need to do in order to meet the demands of potential positions.

Assessing Potential

Anyone who has struggled to identify, assess and predict future performance will understand how difficult this is. For many people, the idea that you could predict with any degree of accuracy which of the qualities an individual is demonstrating today will equip that same person for future senior management would raise serious questions. Predicting who will become the senior managers of the future has been an issue of concern for many.

Competencies offer another way of looking at the prediction of potential. A key reason for this is that they place the focus less on the individual and the qualities they demonstrate, than on what competencies will be required in the future for managing at a senior level. In other words, they help us to approach the problem from another, perhaps more fruitful, angle.

Where a set of competencies has been identified they can often be expressed in terms of their application at different levels in the organisation. In practice this means that potential can be assessed in relation to the level of performance required in the current job, the level of performance required in a job one level above and the level of performance required at a more senior level.

Some organisations have applied this approach in three or four levels which could work as follows. An overall set of competencies is identified which applies to the jobs in a particular part of the organisation. The application of the competencies might work like this:

Level 1, entry – seeks to identify how the competencies need to be demonstrated in action to achieve superior performance at entry level.

Level 2, manager – seeks to identify how the competencies need to be demonstrated in action, to achieve superior performance as a manager.

Level 3, department manager – seeks to identify how the competencies need to be demonstrated to achieve superior performance as a department manager.

Level 4, head of function – seeks to identify how the competencies need to be demonstrated to achieve superior performance as head of function.

This enables a sophisticated level of discrimination to be applied to assessing competencies at different levels, resulting in a greater ability to assess potential.

In some organisations, every manager undergoes an assessment of potential every few years. Assessments are usually based on profiles of managers at various levels in the organisation. The profiles will usually concentrate on the general competencies but may also include areas such as specific job or professional competence. Such assessments can be done as part of an extended appraisal process using upward and sometimes 360 degree appraisal. Such assessments are frequently used as part of a wider development centre.

Whichever way the assessment is carried out, it should always lead to a clearly defined plan of action for development.

Succession Planning

Getting each of the above in place, effective recruitment and selection, improved approaches to training and development and better processes for assessment of potential, greatly helps with succession planning.

Succession planning is essentially about ensuring that the organisation can put in place the right person in the right job at the right time. A process which defines and applies competencies can greatly assist.

In practical terms, those responsible for succession planning can maintain a clear picture of the future personnel needs of the organisation matched against the competencies required for each key position. Having identified the competencies can greatly assist understanding of the jobs which need to be filled. Providing that regular assessments are conducted, they will also have access to information about potential candidates who meet the competency requirements. It remains then for the succession planners to bring the two key elements of this process together as required.

Managing Performance

One of the real benefits which many line managers identify themselves which is to be gained from competencies has to do with the increased information it provides for managing performance.

We referred in Chapter 2 of this report to the importance of understanding what performance is, if it is to be measured properly. Clearly defined competencies greatly assist this understanding.

By far the most popular method of managing performance in most organisations remains the appraisal, although in many cases this now takes place more frequently than the traditional once a year. Appraisal has also taken on new forms in many organisations, with a large number introducing upward appraisal, in which members of teams conduct an appraisal for their team leader. An increasing number of organisations have taken this to the next stage and use a process of 360 degree appraisal. This involves a range of colleagues, peers and customers in conducting an appraisal for an individual, usually a manager or senior professional.

For both upward and 360 degree appraisal to be effective, it is necessary to have a clearly defined set of measures and, of course, competencies provide an ideal basis for constructing these.

In a majority of organisations the process for managing performance is generally as follows:

A Performance Review Process

The objectives of performance review are:

- to ensure that every individual is aware of what they are expected to achieve in their job

- to make them aware of how they can achieve this and what help is available

- to help each individual to think about their own development needs and prepare a plan for achieving these.

For the implementation of performance review, each individual:

- agrees a number of targets or objectives to be achieved during the year. The emphasis is frequently on 'agreeing', rather than having them imposed

- is made aware of their key result areas, the outputs required from their job and the standards of performance to be achieved

- is made aware of the competencies which are required of them to achieve their job outputs through superior performance

- is made aware of how their role and function contributes to the overall aims and mission of the organisation

- agrees to prepare a Personal Development Plan

- receives a regular review and feedback on progress from their manager. Such sessions are generally more open than may have been the case traditionally and usually involve a high degree of self appraisal.

The final part of the process is an overall annual review when plans and achievements for the year are reviewed and re-laid for the following year.

Each of the above elements are typical ways in which organisations use competencies as a part of changing the way the organisation works.

Other Uses of Competencies

Broadly speaking, the applications we describe above cover the most important ways in which organisations use competencies. Most other uses could be described as flowing out of those above.

Many organisations which are seeking to bring about changes in culture see the development of competencies as helping to push the process of culture change forward. We would not describe competencies as a tool for culture change, but we would suggest that the application of competencies can support other processes of culture change. Competencies are likely to require that more attention is placed on recognising what contributes to superior performance, therefore helping to bring into the open more objective and open forms of assessment. Openness and objectivity are both characteristics which contribute to changes in culture.

Record Keeping

As people in the organisation are assessed in relation to the competency profile it will be important to identify and maintain a record of the competencies achieved by individuals across the company. A well maintained and up-to-date database of competencies of individual employees in the company will be an invaluable tool in the application of some of the key subject areas of this chapter, including succession planning, redeployment, training and development and assessing potential. Such a database will inform effective and speedy decision making on a range of issues for which in many organisations information is not generally available.

A not unusual occurrence is for an operational manager to need urgently an individual with a particular set of skills for a project or task. In many instances the organisation is unable to meet this requirement because there are no accurate records of individual competencies. This leads to anger and dissatisfaction with the way records are kept, usually by the human resource function.

The Leaderless Team

A further example where the maintenance of an effective database can provide valuable information is in the creation of project teams and in many instances grouping people together to undertake a task in what has fashionably come to be called a leaderless team. Generally speaking this refers to a group of people who have been tasked to do a particular job which will be monitored and rewarded on the basis of what the team achieves, not what a leader achieves. Leaderless teams are becoming increasingly popular in organisations which are seeking to involve and empower all employees in pursuit of continuous improvement, quicker decision making and the ability to respond more quickly to meeting customer requirements.

In building such teams and, for that matter, any team, it will be increasingly important to be able to make an informed selection of members based on a knowledge of the competencies they bring. It is well accepted that the most effective teams are likely to be made up of people with a range of skills, knowledge and attitudes, people who naturally learn to accept and play different roles in aiding the team to achieve success.

A database of competencies can provide the detailed information which will enable the selection of team members to be made on a much more informed basis than just relying on information which is or is not in files and heads.

Competencies can bring significant benefit to an organisation and can be used in a variety of ways. In addition to the ways we have identified in this report, we are confident that individual organisations will be using competencies to improve performance in ways which we are currently unaware of.

7 The pitfalls and potential barriers in using competencies

Some organisations spend a year or more conducting competency studies, defining competencies for jobs at every level in the organisation, including all specialist roles. The outputs, clusters of knowledge skills and attributes, then inform decisions about all Human Resource issues – recruitment and selection, training and development, career and succession planning, and so on. All are vital issues to the future success of any organisation and all deserve better-informed decision making.

A poorly planned, or poorly executed study may well result in inadequate, incomplete or even incorrect definition of the organisation-specific competencies. This will mean that all those vital 'people decisions' are made against the wrong criteria; one can imagine the ramifications, not least for whoever initiated the whole competency study!

Following the steps and recommendations contained in this report, should provide a sound basis for progress. There are bound to be some challenges along the way. Obstacles are a test of conviction, that the outcome is worth achieving. Yet, all sound project planning includes the anticipation of pitfalls and barriers, then taking steps to avoid or overcome them.

We list below some of the issues to be considered, together with (where appropriate) suggested solutions.

Barriers in the Organisational Climate or Culture

When considering the organisational fit, a major challenge is presented if there are no defined 'Organisational Competencies'. There should, ideally, be a clear link between individual competencies and the organisation's core competencies – the things that the organisation is good at, that give it competitive advantage. Where core competencies have been defined and broadcast internally, it is likely that many HR/HRD activities are already aligned. People are probably hired on the basis of (loosely) matching these competencies, leading to achievement of vision and goals. Training activity is also likely to be tied in, in a similar way.

If the organisation does not have an articulated vision, mission, overarching strategy and identified core competencies, it may well be preferable to facilitate these elements, first. It has been argued that, without these foundations, to concentrate on individual competencies is pointless. Where these organisational elements have been identified, then many clues for the subsequent competency studies will be found under headings such as Vision, Mission, Core Competencies, Values, Key Result Areas and Critical Success Factors.

If the organisation is going through a period of major / rapid change, some will argue that a competency study which takes some months to complete will be out of date before it has produced any outputs. There can be truth in this, particularly if the studies only concentrate on what differentiates today's high performers from the average or poor. A different set of competencies might be in demand, once work has reached implementation stage. This scenario, above all others, calls for a clear focus on the performers of the future. The early interviews with senior managers and strategic thinkers will need to be more probing. This audience will need to be able to:

- detail the difference in outputs that will be required from the manager/performer of the future

- say what are the new challenges their people are likely to face

- describe the different knowledge, skills and attributes that will be required to determine success in the future.

Some organisational climates inhibit, rather than promote, continuous improvement and high performance through increased motivation. Stringer and Litwin of Harvard Graduate Business School identified seven primary determinants of organisational climate:

- Mission and Strategy

- Leadership and Management

- Values and Beliefs

- Rewards and Recognition

- Systems and Structure

- Knowledge and Skills

- The External Environment.

Of these, Leadership and Management were established to be responsible for over 70% of the climate ("How it feels, to work around here"), following extensive research. The good news here is that competency studies and approaches should ultimately improve performance in these areas. On the down side, there are seven remaining determinants which may each hold inhibiting factors, working against the success of a competency project.

A 'blame' culture is typified by people focusing on doing things right, rather than doing the right things. It may be difficult to identify the potential high flyers, when only the reckless have their heads above the parapet. As one HR executive put it, "..we recognise the value of having wild ducks, but we do like ours to fly in formation..". When challenged, most (if not all) senior managers recognise that it is healthy to adopt a stance of learning from mistakes that follow calculated risk-taking, based on sound judgement. If that is the case, then they should 'go public', to liberate the potential for superior performance. It is all part of becoming a 'learning organisation'.

Where there is an inward-looking climate, than an internally-driven competency study might draw completely incorrect conclusions about true superior performance. Some organisations grow steadily, despite focusing on the 'wrong' things. Their 'success' derives from critical mass, inertia, unique products, a monopolistic situation, one corner of the business holding the rest up, or for several other reasons. Where this has been identified, part of the solution may be to involve external customers in defining the competencies.

In autocratic, hierarchical organisations, it may be difficult to define superior performance. It may be necessary to first determine where the autocracy stops, then measure differences at various levels. The use of an employee attitude survey could be considered, if acceptable to senior management.

Conflicting styles at the top. In some organisations, there is a relaxed, liberated and liberating executive at the top, greeted by smiles wherever he or she goes in the organisation. That leader might be blissfully unaware that, at the next level down, there is the real power-base effectively running a dictatorship. In these circumstances, the desired competencies agreed to by the 'highest decision maker' stand no chance of implementation if the dictator/s does not agree. It then becomes vital to involve the second level in all discussions and decision-making, facilitating agreement on areas where there is common ground. This scenario demands more emphasis on the business benefits to be gained from a competency approach, including cost / benefit analysis.

Low employee trust levels. In an organisation that has recently experienced considerable downsizing or delayering activity, one can expect a high level of mistrust around any new management initiative. In one recent staff survey we conducted, the CEO and HR professionals were convinced that everyone in the organisation understood the business reasons for the previous year's redundancies, and that all would agree they were handled fairly and sensitively. So convinced were they, that they insisted that two questions be included in the confidential questionnaire, to ratify their questions. They saw it as a great PR opportunity to report positive scores on these issues, when giving feedback to staff on the collated survey responses. They had to modify their plans, on discovering that the vast majority of staff 'strongly disagreed' with their positive statements. Many respondents even interpreted the inclusion of the questions as an indication that more mass redundancies were imminent. Needless to say, every organisation will face different issues in such circumstances. In all, however, there will be a need for widespread, open communication before embarking on a competency project.

Hidden norms. It may be part of the organisational culture, that certain behaviours or attributes are necessary, in order to progress (or even get recruited). These may be unspoken 'norms', which would never appear in a published list of corporate values. Even if they are unsound as predictors of high performance, it would be unwise to ignore them. Depending on your degree of conviction, you may choose to construct your competency studies to include comparisons between those who do not possess these qualities. Be cautious here. There may be a danger of you discriminating against, just because of a perception that others discriminate in favour.

There are many other potential issues to be faced, when considering the climate and culture of an organisation. We trust that the six scenarios outlined above will provide some thoughts on how to manage others. Make full use of any data available, such as recent staff surveys, upward appraisal exercises, customer research and so on. Be aware, also, that the introduction of a competency-based approach is a cultural change in itself. Just as with any change, sensitive handling is required and effective communication will be the key.

Avoiding a Bureaucratic Nightmare

As we have warned elsewhere, one of the biggest dangers can stem from allowing the competency project to develop a life of its own.

In Chapter 4, we looked at defining what you are seeking to achieve and setting clear objectives for the analysis. If senior management have become excited about the many benefits to be gained from a competency approach, the result might be a multi-faceted, organisation-wide project aimed at influencing change in every people-related activity, in every corner of the business. In a dynamic business environment, there is a danger of losing focus, on changing business objectives.

Faced with this scenario, we recommend:

- **Start with a pilot.** Agree on a strategically-important area of business, where (initially, at least) only one or two applications will be tested (say, recruitment plus some targeted training and development).

- **Ensure the outcomes will be readily measurable.** An ideal target audience for a pilot study is often regarded to be the sales function. Their outputs are obviously measurable, the competency approach can usually be integrated with ease and it is often in the sales environment where expensive new recruits move on, for various reasons. Get it right, and the tangible benefits from the pilot may well pay for the rest of the competency studies. If management competencies are the sole target for organisation-wide activity, then sales managers could be targeted for a pilot.

- **Measure, evaluate and prove value.** This pilot group, apart from validating the worth of the whole project, may well become the organisation's 'Champions of Change'.

- **Gain senior management commitment to the whole project.** Redefine boundaries, priorities and expectations, as appropriate. Include all the cost implications.

- **Publicise the results widely.** Ensure that everyone understands the potential benefits, after a 'live' pilot in their own organisation, rather than by paying lip-service to results achieved elsewhere. Pay close attention to any sceptical line managers, whose full commitment and cooperation will be vital, later.

- **Build a full Project Plan.** Adopt structures and techniques as one would for any major project. Be precise about resource and time requirements, boundaries, objectives, deliverables and dependencies. Try to ensure that all business units, representative line managers and key specialist functions are represented, even if only on relevant sub-projects.

- **Extend research analysis, to avoid duplication.** Try not to involve the same target audience in more than one analysis method, during each phase of the work. If necessary, extend the depth of the research, to inform more than one intended application.

- **Gain agreement to resource requirements.** Make sure that the study is viable, includes the right number and level of targets, and will provide reliable data.

- **Inform, inform, inform.** Keep senior management advised of progress (Reporting arrangements should have been agreed within the project plan), keep the project team motivated and keep line management / affected staff continuously updated. Everyone who is involved in the research phase needs to know what is expected of them, how long it will take, why they are doing it and what the potential benefits are.

- **Plan the work, then work the plan.** (See Chapter 8 on implementation.)

Pitfalls With Analysis

The major pitfall at analysis stage is that – through budget or resource restrictions – the survey target group is too small to provide a truly representative sample. The reverse scenario can also present a problem, where the subjects are many and diverse, presenting difficulty in arriving at a set of common, differentiating competencies.

Job effectiveness criteria should be used to identify a selection of high performers, against whom a selection of average performers needs to be compared. To match some objectives, it may also be necessary to identify some below-average performers (to determine minimum acceptable performance levels for new entrants, etc., or to assess common training/development needs). In some organisations, it is very difficult for line managers to admit that they might be carrying below average or incompetent performers. ("We operate as a high-performance team, with complementary skills and attributes." "All of our people are good; the below-average have either been developed to be fully effective, or moved out.") When faced with this response, it is necessary to first agree that all might be classified as 'good', but that it is necessary to identify some who are more good than the pack rather than some who are less good.

Another issue frequently faced when asking line managers to identify high performers is that of personal prejudice or favour. Some probing is necessary, to identify the reasons behind line managers' selection. It may be that some genuine high performers have been overlooked, in favour of those who share the same interests or attitudes of the boss. Senior managers often seek to 'clone' themselves, especially when succession planning is on the agenda. Test the selections against several criteria, then choose those subjects who rate highly against them all. If the integrity of the exercise is in doubt, it may be necessary to suggest several selection approaches (e.g. peers, subordinates, customers, etc.).

Here are some further challenges and issues that might be faced during the analysis phase:

- **Ignoring 'the obvious'.** In many jobs, some basic knowledge, skills and attributes can be ignored for the purpose of defining competencies (for example, basic numeracy and literacy skills). Do not take this premise too far. In the case of the bank teller example earlier in this report, all the interpersonal skills, behaviours and attitudes may be in place, but the teller would never be considered a superior performer if the till failed to balance every night.

- **Time and expense.** Some analysis methods are more time-consuming than others. For example, a face-to-face meeting to explore critical incidents might well take up to two hours, plus a further two to analyse. There may also be costs associated with transcribing a taped interview.

- **Interviewer expertise.** Internal interviewers may well need to be trained, to maintain quality and consistency vital to the success of the research phase.

- **Missed job tasks.** Again, if the focus is on critical incidents, some less important (though still relevant) aspects may not get included in the analysis.

- **Survey results are only as good as the surveyor.** Ideally, surveys should not be used as the first (or only) data collection method. The survey results will only reflect the questions asked, which may result in key areas and competencies being missed. The survey is an inexpensive method for collecting large volumes of data; it should be preceded by some qualitative work, to aid the survey construction.

Barriers to Usage

Once the concepts have been understood and accepted (and provided you follow the steps recommended in this report), senior management usually remain committed to the competency approach, unless line managers convince them that usage will be too unwieldy or if the length and cost of the research phase gets out of hand.

Common causes of resistance and blockages are:

- **Jargon.** Perhaps with the aid of user panels before launch, it is vital to keep the language simple and in terms familiar to the organisation.

- **Ineffective communication.** We have stressed several times in this report the need to fully brief – up, down and across the organisation. Failure to do so, particularly on changes to expect and benefits associated with the changes, can cause people to remain in 'denial' stages of the change process.

- **Lack of cohesion with organisational values and norms.** Competencies must fit with, not conflict with, the business values, culture, mission, etc. Any mismatch will possibly cause rejection.

- **Exposure.** There will be some, including line managers, who fear that the new approach will expose their own under-performance. People at all levels will need support and training, to maintain commitment and enthusiasm.

Avoiding the Pitfalls and Overcoming the Barriers

Where appropriate, tactics have been suggested to meet all of the potential difficulties outlined in this chapter. Other, more general advice, follows:

- Try to understand the organisational culture / climate, before embarking on a competency study. Broad research invested at the front end will pay dividends when it comes to interpreting the research.

- Where senior managers say "It is difficult to define our culture", ask some probing questions based on 'What if...' scenarios. If necessary, include some culture / climate questions in the research, to establish organisational norms.

- Ensure that the whole exercise is scoped and planned along common Project Management guidelines. If necessary, enlist some help from inside or outside the organisation. The resource investment will be worthwhile, in terms of structured, guaranteed outcomes.

- Choose an appropriate mix of analysis methods. The more often that competencies are identified by different research approaches, the more certain it will be that a differentiating competency has been identified. Remember though that this is the most expensive phase. Do not engage in costly research just for the sake of it ('paralysis by analysis'). There may be a much more cost effective way to collect substantive data, for example by questionnaire to a wider selection of job-holders, to validate earlier findings.

- Generally, try to conduct face-to-face research with 1.5 times as many high performers as average performers. Experience tells that there is most to learn from the high flyers. Less than 15 - 20 subjects for each job study sample may not allow for any quantitative comparisons.

- Enlist the support of key decision makers, influencers and specialists as early as practicable in the project. Ownership equals commitment.

- Do not walk away from the project (or even step back), once the implementation stage has been reached. Advice and support may well be required by the new 'owners' and it will be vital to look for signs of any barriers to usage, any reversion to the status quo.

- Remain sensitive to the issues faced by those (particularly line managers) who may not have been exposed to performance measurement of this nature before.

8 A practical plan for implementation

Do Competencies Add Value?

The answer to this question has of course to be a resounding yes, followed by the inevitable but. The yes, as we trust we have demonstrated in this report, refers to the value an organisation will get from taking a more considered, structured and informed approach to issues such as recruitment and selection, training and development, succession planning and managing performance. The but comes from evidence we have seen that some people want to apply a competency approach but think it can be done without making the necessary commitment of time and resources.

We trust that in your reading of this report you will have gained an understanding of what competencies are and how they work. We trust also that you will have realised that to make them a successful and valuable addition to the range of tools and techniques available for achieving organisational success, they must be robust, relevant, flexible and user friendly.

Competencies only add value if they:

- are understood by all,

- referred to by managers to assist them in doing their job and

- are seen to be playing an active part in the life of the organisation.

Sitting on a shelf, gathering dust alongside procedures manuals, they add little or no value.

Making Competencies Work For You

Competencies can be a powerful tool helping you to make the organisation more effective and successful. If you want them to add value, we suggest that you need to think carefully about the following:

- Why do you plan to introduce competencies?

- What are you seeking to achieve, as a result of introducing them?

- Are you prepared to make the necessary investment of time and resources, to ensure that the competencies you develop are relevant to your organisational need, also robust enough to stand up to the scrutiny of managers and employees? In other words, will they work in the real world?

- Do you have the support and commitment of senior line management?

How to Apply Competencies in Your Organisation

Applying competencies requires a commitment of time and effort from the organisation and because of this, it is important to be clear what will be involved and what the organisation will get out of the process from the start.

A useful beginning is to start a debate in the organisation about competencies. Most people will have heard about competencies, but there may be some uncertainty about what they are and how they work. They are considered by some to be just another management fad, much like all of the others, which will go away in time.

This debate should get people thinking about what competencies are, how they work and what they can do for an organisation. It should seek to raise awareness and get people talking.

The debate will need to be stimulated and informed, so it will be useful to feed in information about why other organisations develop and apply competencies, as well as how they do it. It should also seek to help people to understand what the organisation will gain from a competency approach.

As we said in Chapter 4, organisations decide to adopt a competency approach for a wide variety of reasons including:

- to improve the effectiveness of recruitment and selection

- to improve the way they manage performance

- to help ensure that the training and development process is aligned with the needs of the business

- to encourage employees to use Personal Development Plans

- to assist with a culture change process

- to help align the human resource function with the business

- to help measure manager and employee effectiveness

- to help employees understand the essential elements for success doing their job.

If the debate creates a heightened interest in competencies, the organisation can then move on to considering in more detail the need for developing a competency approach. Some more specific questions about how the organisation could apply competencies and what they would expect to get out of this approach can be considered. We suggest that the following questions be considered:

- What do you want competencies to do for you?

- How do you envisage that competencies will contribute to improved business performance?

- Will competencies be used as part of a wider process of culture change?

Answers to these and other questions which will be raised are contained in the text of this report, which should help to answer most questions which people have about competencies.

A Plan for Implementing Competencies

Once a decision has been made to go ahead with defining and implementing competencies it is advisable to put together a plan for implementation. The detail of the plan will of necessity be developed in each organisation and geared to meeting the actual needs and expectations of that organisation. However, it is possible to provide some broad outlines for what a plan should cover. We suggest the following outline approach.

Establish a small working party

- A small working party representative of the organisation as a whole should be established. For this group to be effective, it is important that the members are drawn from all the main business units. It is equally important to ensure that there is strong representation of line management.

Set clear objectives

- It is essential to identify a clear set of objectives covering what the organisation plans to get out of the investment of time and effort in developing competencies. The objectives will be organisational specific but should cover:

    – why the organisation is developing competencies

    – how competencies will be used

    – what are the specific outputs and achievements which can be expected?

    – who will competencies apply to?

    – how will the development and implementation of competencies be monitored?

    – how will success be measured?

- At this stage it will also be important to clarify what the competencies will cover. As has been outlined earlier in this report competencies generally cover a range of generic skills, knowledge, and behaviour, but could also include technical and professional competencies required as part of the professional occupation of a job holder.

- The working party also needs to consider what they propose to do about the definition of competencies. Will they use as a starting point some of the competencies which have been identified by other organisations such as the Management Charter Initiative (MCI), or do they propose to develop their own organisational specific competencies? In reaching the decision it is useful to remember that whichever way competencies are defined, either by taking and adapting an existing set or developing a new set, those which are agreed must be relevant to the needs of the business.

- It will be important for the competencies approach to have a clear orientation on the future. In identifying competencies is necessary to make sure that they apply to the way people manage in the future not the way they managed in the past.

- Adopting a competency approach is not just setting up another way of improving training within the organisation. Training will be a part of a competencies approach but will not be the reason for it. Competencies will have an impact on the way the business is run – on performance, on recruitment and on training and development.

- The working party should consider whether or not to involve a consultant to assist with the process, not necessarily to come along and design the competencies, but to generally advise on the process. External experience can bring many insights and help an organisation to avoid many pitfalls.

Communicate the plan and intentions

- In developing competencies it is important to involve a wide range of people and at the same time inform everyone about what is going on. If the benefits which an organisation will gain from the development and implementation of competencies are clear, everyone needs to be informed about why this approach is being adopted.

- An ongoing part of the implementation should be a plan for communication. Effective communication is required at all levels, to all managers and employees. It should start early in the process, informing all concerned that competencies are being identified, what they are and how they will be applied. During the development phase it will be important to involve, inform and consult as wide a range of people as possible.

- Once the development phase has been completed, full information about competencies and how they will be used throughout the organisation should be widely published.

How to identify and define the competencies

A key issue for the working party is to decide how they will identify and define the competencies. We recommend using a number of methods of analysis. Using a management survey will provide a good framework and set of competencies; on its own, it will not test the robustness of the competencies and how they will be used in practice. We recommend the following approach:

- Brainstorm and debate with a small group of well informed people to establish the first draft of a framework and set of competencies.

- Conduct a management survey (as outlined in Chapter 2 of this report) to assess and refine the framework and set of competencies; revise them and amend as necessary.

- Take the framework and set of competencies and apply at least one, and probably two, of the following methods of analysis to test the robustness of the competencies in action:

  - role-modelling

  - critical-incident technique

  - in-depth interviews

  - repertory grid

  - a competency analysis workshop.

  These additional methods of analysis, each of which is outlined in Chapter 5 of this report, will allow the competencies which have been defined, to be tested in the real world where they have to be applied and make sense to the people using them.

- On completion of this analysis the working party can be reasonably confident that they have developed a robust framework and set of competencies which can be applied in the organisation.

- In some organisations it may be necessary at this stage to refer back to senior management for them to approve the final version of the competencies. This will be no bad thing and even if this is not required, it will be important to make sure that senior management are kept involved and informed in the process. The support and commitment of senior management is essential in the development and application of competencies.

Implementation

The framework and competencies have now been defined. The next stage is to communicate them as widely as possible across the organisation and then apply them in action. The nature of the implementation element of the plan will depend on how they are to be used. In the first instance it may be necessary to conduct some training. The following proposed implementation plan makes certain assumptions about how competencies are to be used; these are based on the use to which a large number of organisations put competencies. Of course, any plan for implementation needs to be organisation specific and the following is provided as a guide to what could be done.

- **Competency workshops.** The quickest and most effective way of getting the majority of people to understand and buy-in to competencies is to hold a series of competency workshops. The purpose of a competency workshop is to help people understand competencies and appreciate how to apply them in their work. Full details of what the workshop should cover are given in Chapter 6 of this report.

- **Personal Development Plans.** Everyone should be encouraged to take greater responsibility for their own development and the introduction of competencies provides an ideal opportunity for an organisation to introduce a process of personal development planning. This is often done as part of a competency workshop but can just as easily be done as a separate exercise. Further details of personal development planning are given in Chapter 6 of this report.

- **Communication and/or training,** covering how competencies will be linked to performance management through the appraisal system and objective setting. This can also be done during a competency workshop.

- **The preparation of job profiles.** This can be done as a continuing part of the work of the competency working party, as job profiles will need to be developed and prepared for use throughout the organisation.

- **Recruitment and selection.** Some training may be required for recruiters in competency based interviewing skills.

- **The management of change.** Many organisations use the introduction of competencies to put some additional force behind an existing process of culture change. Competencies, providing as they do a new way of looking at performance and behaviour, can be an ideal vehicle for driving changes in culture. Competencies provide a focus on what people do and how they do it, which in turn can be used to provide a sense of direction for the organisation and a focal point for a change in the culture.

Monitor, Review and Evaluate

An essential element in the successful implementation of competencies will be monitoring and evaluating how effective they have been in bringing about the changes which it was predicted they would. In developing the plan for identification, definition and implementation, the competency working party will have identified how competencies are to be used in the organisation. As a part of this process we suggest that they should also establish a plan and method for evaluation.

We propose the following guideline approach to evaluation:

- **Short-term evaluation.** This should seek to establish if the competencies are being used, how they are being used and is the current use effective?

- **Medium-term evaluation.** This will take place in the medium term which we define as at least six months after implementation through to eighteen months. By this time it should be possible to identify the impact and some of the achievements. It should look at usage and effectiveness

- **Long-term evaluation.** This will explore what impact competencies have had on business performance. This type of evaluation cannot be done until some two years after implementation and will seek to identify what impact competencies have had on recruitment and selection, performance management, culture and personal development plans.

Evaluation will only be truly effective if is linked back to the objectives which were set during the development phase. If clear objectives have not been set it is very difficult to assess what has been achieved.

A useful additional way of evaluating the impact of competencies is see if it is possible to benchmark what has been done and what has been achieved with similar activities in other organisations. A brief guide to benchmarking competencies is given in Chapter 5 of this report. Benchmarking with other organisations provides comparison and insight and can be used at any stage in the competency process; when used as part of evaluation it can provide a way of assessing what has been achieved and also act as a stimulus to renewed effort.

We trust that, if you have used this report and other references wisely, you will then choose to offer your organisation for benchmarking comparison. We naturally trust and believe that, if you do, you will then find that many more of your processes and outcomes fall under the heading 'Agreed Best Practice', than under headings for future improvements required.

Bibliography

Choi, Chong, Ju; Kelemen, Mihaela (1995) *Cultural Competences: managing co-operatively across cultures*, Dartmouth.

Hirsh, Wendy; Strebler, Marie (1994) Defining managerial skills and competences, *Gower Handbook of Management Development*, Fourth Edition, Ed. Alan Mumford, Gower, London.

Katzenbach, Jon R, Smith, Douglas K (1993) *The Wisdom of Teams*, Harvard Business School Press, Boston, Massachusetts, USA.

MCI (1991) *Occupational Standards for Managers, Management 1 and Assessment Guidance*, London.

Semler, R. (1993) *Maverick*, Arrow Business Books, London.

Sparrow, Paul, (1995) Organisational Competencies: A valid approach for the future? *International Journal of Selection and Recruitment,* Vol. 3, No. 3, July 1995.

Spencer, Lyle; Spencer, Signe (1993) *Competence at Work*, John Wiley & Sons, New York.

The Assessment of Management Competencies (1990) Council for National Academic Awards Business and Technician Education Council, London.

The Industrial Society (1996) *Management Competencies*, Managing Best Practice No. 21, The Industrial Society, London.